GLBTQ

The Survival Guide for
Gay, Lesbian, Bisexual,
Transgender, and
Questioning Teens

GLBTQ

The Survival Guide for Gay, Lesbian, Bisexual, Transgender, and Questioning Teens

Revised & Updated Second Edition

Kelly Huegel

free spirit
PUBLISHING®

Library of Congress Cataloging-in-Publication Data
Huegel, Kelly, 1974–
        GLBTQ : the survival guide for gay, lesbian, bisexual, transgender, and questioning teens / Kelly Huegel. — Rev. & updated 2nd ed.
            p. cm.
        Includes bibliographical references and index.
        ISBN 978-1-57542-363-0
    1. Homosexuality—United States—Juvenile literature. 2. Coming out (Sexual orientation)—United States—Juvenile literature. 3. Gay teenagers—United States—Juvenile literature. 4. Lesbian teenagers—United States—Juvenile literature. 5. Transgender people—United States—Juvenile literature. 6. Bisexuals—United States—Juvenile literature. I. Title. II. Title: Gay, lesbian, bisexual, transgender, questioning.
        HQ76.25.H84 2011
        306.76'6—dc22

                                                                                    2010048196

eBook ISBN: 978-1-57542-704-1

The names of the teens and young adults quoted throughout this book have been changed to protect their privacy and/or safety.

Photo credits: cover © Stockbyte, page 6 © istockphoto.com/Christopher Futcher, page 27 © Rick Friedman/Corbis, page 48 © istockphoto.com/Niko Guido, page 67 © Will & Deni McIntyre/Corbis, page 85 © Yuri Arcurs I Dreamstime.com, page 94 © istockphoto.com/Juan Estey, page 110 © istockphoto.com/johnnyscriv, page 129 © Pavel Losevsky I Dreamstime.com, page 150 © istockphoto.com/Christopher Futcher, page 167 © istockphoto.com/pongpol boonyen, page 189 © Ali Rıza Yıldız I Dreamstime.com

Reading Level Grades 9 & Up; Interest Level Ages 13 & Up;
Fountas & Pinnell Guided Reading Level Z

10 9 8 7 6 5 4 3 2 1
Printed in the United States of America
S18860111

Free Spirit Publishing Inc.
217 Fifth Avenue North, Suite 200
Minneapolis, MN 55401-1299
(612) 338-2068
help4kids@freespirit.com
www.freespirit.com

Dedication

For my family, for whom I have the utmost love and respect.

For Yvonne, who inspires me.

And for queer kids everywhere. You are my heroes.

Acknowledgments

Here is where I get to thank people. I'll do my best not to make this sound like an Oscar speech and will get off the stage before the music starts playing.

Thank you, first, to Yvonne. You have the biggest, most generous heart of anyone I know. You have enriched the lives of so many young people and helped them learn that it doesn't matter where they've come from, but rather where they're going. Your love both humbles and empowers me.

To my family, whose continued support and encouragement truly know no bounds, thank you. If it had been up to me, I could not have chosen better. You are the definition of unconditional love.

Thanks to Free Spirit for still believing in this book and for being a voice for kids on so many issues. An enormous thank you to Douglas Fehlen, my editor, who took such great care in his work and whose contributions helped take this book to the next level. Thanks, as well, to Phoenix Schneider for so kindly agreeing to take part in this second edition.

I wish to thank again all of those who contributed to the first iteration of this book, including the national organizations that provided facts, opinions, and expertise on these varied and sometimes complicated issues. I am just the mouthpiece—you are doing the work.

Finally, again, thank you to the fearless teens and young adults who lent their voices and their very personal stories to this book. You are our future, and that future is very bright, indeed.

Contents

Foreword by Phoenix Schneider

Today is unlike any period in history in terms of the GLBTQ rights movement and our awareness and acceptance of varying orientations and identities. When I was growing up as a teen in the 1990s, I faced some significant challenges with regard to my sexual orientation and gender identity. I first came out as bisexual in high school and felt pressured by both the straight and gay communities to pick a side.

When I came out later in college as trans/genderqueer, both the straight and GLBTQ communities wanted me to pick a gender. People were uncomfortable with the fact that I didn't fall into one nice and neat little box—straight or gay, male or female. What I learned is that there are no limitations to how a person can identify, and no one can take away what feels right for you or the ways in which you choose to express yourself.

Since that time, more people—especially young people—have been pushing the envelope in terms of how they identify. This change is part of a kind of gender and sexuality revolution taking place throughout society. Statistically, today's young people are more accepting not only of GLBTQ people, but also of those who choose not to identify as one gender or sexual orientation over another. These evolving viewpoints encourage a celebration of each person's unique blueprint in this wonderfully diverse universe.

Still, as with all societal change, evolution can be slow and significant challenges remain. Homophobia and transphobia still exist in many communities, and these negative attitudes can have a heavy impact on the safety and well-being of all GLBTQ people, especially queer young people.

Fortunately, there are more resources for queer teens than ever, including this book. *GLBTQ: The Survival Guide for Gay, Lesbian, Bisexual, Transgender, and Questioning Teens* can provide you with different perspectives, ideas, support, and resources about coming out, religion and spirituality, dating and relationships, self-care, and many other issues.

This book takes a holistic approach to what it's like to be a young lesbian, gay, bisexual, transgender, queer, or questioning person and provides not only sound advice on dealing with common issues, but also voices of queer teens who have "been there." Kelly Huegel has written a guide that can benefit anyone who is GLBTQ or questioning their sexual orientation or gender identity as well as anyone who cares about someone who is GLBTQ.

Much of my own work as program director with The Trevor Project, the leading national organization focused on crisis and suicide prevention efforts among GLBTQ teens, is focused on helping young people with limited support systems and access to resources. The Trevor Project fosters creative self-expression, support, and acceptance for all, regardless of sexual orientation or gender identity or expression.

If you are a young GLBTQ person who feels misunderstood, lonely, depressed, or suicidal, you are not alone. Whether you are gay, lesbian, bisexual, transgender, or feel like you don't really identify with one particular sexual orientation or gender identity, *this is normal.* Know that there are people in this world who understand and accept you for exactly who you are. You can connect with other GLBTQ people and straight allies who are more than willing to provide advice and support.

It's truly a journey to fully accept and discover who you are, how you relate to others, and what decisions empower you to feel most comfortable being who you were born to be: *your unique, beautiful self.*

Phoenix Schneider, MSW
Program Director, The Trevor Project
www.TheTrevorProject.org

Introduction

Dealing with the realization that you are or might be gay, lesbian, bisexual, transgender, or questioning (GLBTQ) can be a real challenge. And I know just how it feels. By the time I was in high school, I was convinced I was somehow different from everyone else, and not in a good way. But GLBTQ people weren't visible where I came from, so the idea that I was a lesbian hadn't taken shape for me. I just hadn't met the right guy yet—the one who would make me start daydreaming of a perfect wedding like many of my friends were doing.

When I got to college, I finally met some people who were GLBTQ and out. Looking at them was like holding up a mirror to myself. My feelings started to make sense, like I'd finally found the missing piece to a big puzzle. But the thought that I might actually be a lesbian frightened me a lot. What would my family and friends say? How could I live "that kind" of life? Feeling hopeless—terrified to tell anyone what I was going through—I decided the only way to escape the conflict and pain I was experiencing was to end my life.

So one night I took an overdose of pills. But as I looked at myself in the mirror, something happened. From somewhere deep inside me I heard a voice that told me I had to live. That no matter what happened, no matter how hard my life was going to be, it was a life worth living. I asked someone to take me to the hospital and, fortunately, we made it there in time.

> This book often uses the word *queer.* This term was once used as a slur to harass or demean GLBTQ people. While it is still used by some in this way, queer is now a word that many GLBTQ people view and use in a positive way. For more information on GLBTQ terminology, see Chapter 1 (page 7).

Now, nearly a decade later, my life is completely different. I have the love and support of my family. I have a wonderful partner. Life is challenging at times, but I'm grateful to have it. I feel very fortunate when I remember that I could have missed out on all of the incredible experiences I've had so far.

The journey from being a confused, scared teen to the out and proud person I am today was a road traveled not by big leaps, but instead by many small steps. As I've grown more accepting of myself, I've been able to get involved with helping other GLBTQ people and their families learn to love and accept themselves and each other. Through my work with PFLAG (Parents, Families and Friends of Lesbians and Gays) and opportunities I've had because of this book, I've talked to young people terrified about coming out and to parents upset about children who have just told them they're GLBTQ. It's been amazing to watch these teens and families go from confusion and anger to acceptance and even joy about who they are.

A Changing World

As a GLBTQ teen, life can sometimes feel pretty lonely. It's easy to think no one cares about what you're going through, but people do care. All over the world, GLBTQ people, parents, friends, family members, and politicians are working to promote understanding and acceptance of those who are gay, lesbian, bisexual, transgender, and questioning. A lot of these efforts are focused on helping teens. PFLAG has made school safety one of its primary concerns. The Gay, Lesbian and Straight Education Network (GLSEN) is focused entirely on improving the school environment for GLBTQ students. The Gay and Lesbian Alliance Against Defamation (GLAAD) is fighting for more positive and accurate messages about queer people in the media.

These are just a few examples. Everyday people at other national and local organizations are making extraordinary progress in fighting for your rights. They're educating school boards, principals, teachers, and other school staff. They're holding in-school workshops and lobbying for better legislation at state capitols and in Washington, D.C. Progress is being made gradually. Life for GLBTQ people is getting better.

This book's first edition was published in 2003. A lot has changed since then—so much so that this revision became necessary. That means there's been progress. Not only are there many new resources for GLBTQ teens, but a lot of legislation protecting the civil rights of queer people has been created. And forget dancing around the topic "civil unions," now we're engaged in a full-on push for marriage rights.

This second edition is fully revised to reflect advances in GLBTQ rights. The sections I was most excited to update, though, are less tangible than facts and figures. They have to do with the changing attitudes among GLBTQ and straight teens.

Today's queer teens are far more likely to be open-minded and have a broad view of sexuality and gender expression. Many young people choose not to label themselves as gay, lesbian, bisexual, or transgender. Instead they may identify as "pansexual," "omnisexual," "genderqueer," or just "other." This change in the way teens refer to themselves reflects an increased openness to nontraditional ideas of sexuality and gender identity.

Perspectives also have changed among straight teens. Overall, they are more accepting of GLBTQ peers (even though sometimes it might not feel like that). The impact of these attitudes on society as young people grow older and, eventually, inherit the world is exciting to contemplate. Communities will become even more accepting of all people—GLBTQ and straight alike.

You might be thinking, "That's great, but what about right now? What about *my* school?" It's easy to say that everything will be okay someday, that this is just part of growing up. But those kinds of reassurances don't help you very much right now.

That's why I originally wrote this book. I remember very clearly what it was like—the worries, insecurities, fears. One moment you might be upset about the grade you got on a quiz, the next you're thinking about big questions like what you want to do with your life. And what if, on top of all that, you suddenly discover you're attracted to someone of the same sex? Or what if you dread changing for gym class because you're in the boys' locker room, but inside you've always felt more like a girl?

Discovering that you might be GLBTQ is a big revelation, and accepting it is a process. One thing that can help in that process is information. This book can't answer all of your questions or counter all of the misinformation and outright lies you may have heard about being GLBTQ. It does, however, have a lot of insight and advice you might not have found anywhere else.

About This Book

What will you find in *GLBTQ: The Survival Guide for Gay, Lesbian, Bisexual, Transgender, and Questioning Teens*? For starters, you'll read information from experts in psychology, sociology, and health care. These authorities offer a lot of insight about what it means to be queer. You'll also find advice from people who work with national organizations advocating for GLBTQ rights, tips for coming out, ideas for creating a more accepting school environment, and help for a variety of other issues and situations.

This book also features true stories from teens and young adults who've been through situations you might be facing. Some of these stories may be very different from your own; others might seem to come from a page right out of your own life. These words from young people can offer support and real-life advice, and so can the books and websites suggested throughout the book.

I wrote this book with all GLBTQ teens in mind. It's my hope that you'll find it helpful, whether you're secure with your sexual orientation or gender identity or just starting to explore these ideas. It's important to remember that when it comes to questions about being GLBTQ, there aren't a lot of cut-and-dry answers. Because every GLBTQ person is an individual, it's difficult to provide answers that are appropriate for everyone. Even in the GLBTQ community there isn't always agreement on details surrounding certain issues. This book offers commonly accepted answers, as well as suggestions for how you can find answers to your own questions.

GLBTQ is meant to be a handbook—use it as you need it. You might read the book from cover to cover, or you might use the contents and index to guide you to sections addressing just the issues you face. The book is a pressure-free zone. Regardless of where you are in your life, you can read the parts you're ready for. The goal isn't to come up with definitive answers, because some answers might lead to other questions. And that's great. It's all part of getting to know yourself.

Even if you're just questioning or curious, that's okay, too. You never have to pick a label for yourself if you don't want to. Many people choose to identify as queer, or say, "I don't identify. I just am who I am." You may decide you're just questioning right now, and that's fine. The purpose of this book is not to make you choose a label, but to help you get to know yourself and be more comfortable with who you are.

GLBTQ people come in all shapes, sizes, and colors: We are African American, Latino, Caucasian, Native American, Asian, Arab American, and Indian. We are Catholic, Protestant, atheist, Buddhist, agnostic, Unitarian, Hindu, and Muslim. We can be teachers, lawyers, doctors, construction workers, executives, athletes, artists, writers, politicians, and any other type of professional you can imagine. And we are parents, friends, partners, sons, daughters, sisters, brothers, aunts, uncles, and grandparents. GLBTQ people are everywhere, and we can be anything we want to be.

Since the first edition of this book was published I've heard from readers, both young and old, who have in some way been touched by its contents. Whether you have a question or story of your own to share, I welcome you to contact me. I can be reached via email (help4kids@freespirit.com) or at the following address.

Free Spirit Publishing
217 Fifth Avenue North, Suite 200
Minneapolis, MN 55401-1299

All the best to you,
Kelly Huegel

P.S. Do you want updated information on legislation and issues mentioned in this book? Visit the Facebook page for *GLBTQ*. I also provide updates on Twitter @GLBTQguide.

▼ **If You Need Help** . . . While daily life is getting better for GLBTQ people, it can still be incredibly challenging. This can be especially true for young people who may be coming to terms with being queer. If you're feeling depressed or confused, or if you just want to talk to someone, call The Trevor Lifeline at 1-866-4-U-TREVOR (1-866-488-7386). Trained counselors will listen without judgment and provide advice on GLBTQ issues. The call is free, and it won't appear on your phone bill. You can call 24 hours a day, any day of the year. ▼

Chapter 1

GLBTQ 101

We are everywhere.

Maybe you've known for years that you're GLBTQ. Or maybe you are only now beginning to question your sexual orientation or gender identity. Regardless of where you might be coming from, it can help to remember that you're not alone.

Researchers believe that between five and six percent of young people are gay, lesbian, or bisexual. Others identify as transgender or questioning. Widely accepted research concludes that roughly 1 in 10 adults is GLBTQ. Think about these statistics the next time you're at the movies or a football game. Whether you're aware of them or not, it's likely people at your school or in your neighborhood are GLBTQ.

By the Numbers

The census of 2010 was the first to count same-sex couples identifying themselves as spouses. Prior to this count, those living in homosexual households were classified as "unmarried partners." The Census Bureau's new designation will provide more accurate data on gay households, which could influence future legislative issues.

Yet many people are uncomfortable talking about differences in sexuality, and that can result in ignorance. You've probably grown up hearing some of the rumors and myths about GLBTQ people. Even the most well-intentioned people can be misinformed about what it means to be queer.

The most powerful response to bias and ignorance is knowledge. This chapter covers the fundamentals of being GLBTQ. Some of what follows might seem like very basic information, but even if you consider yourself knowledgeable about GLBTQ issues, you may be surprised by what you read.

GLBTQ Terminology

One thing that can be confusing about the queer community is the terminology. Sometimes it seems like a whole different language exists. Even among GLBTQ people, there's a lack of consensus about definitions and which words to use when.

For starters, is it GLBTQ, LGBTQ, LGB with T and Q separate? A few decades ago, it was common to say G&L for gay and lesbian. But language evolves as our understanding of GLBTQ people evolves. When the B (for bisexual) was added, the acronym became GLB or LGB. Then the T (for transgender) and Q (for questioning) joined the party.

In this book, you'll see the consistent use of the acronym GLBTQ. When an issue applies specifically to gay, lesbian, bisexual, or transgender people, those specific words will be

▼ **Sexual Orientation and Gender Identity**

The American Psychological Association describes *sexual orientation* as an enduring pattern of emotional, romantic, and/or sexual attraction to men, women, or both sexes. Sexual orientation also refers to an individual's sense of identity based on that pattern.

According to the Sexuality Information and Education Council of the United States, *gender identity* is the internal sense that people have that they are female, male, or some variation of these. For many people, *biological sex*—which is based on chromosomes and sexual anatomy—and *gender identity* are the same. For others, they are different. ▼

used. And although you'll read about people being either GLBTQ or straight, not all transgender people are gay, lesbian, or bisexual. In fact, many transgender people are heterosexual, and some just don't identify with any of the labels. Referring to trans people as GLBTQ doesn't imply that they are necessarily gay, lesbian, or bisexual in their sexual orientations. But the full acronym GLBTQ is used here for consistency.

Another word used often in this book is queer. This word was once used negatively to describe GLBTQ people (and still is, by some). Now, many GLBTQ people and our allies (supporters) use it in a very positive way. For example, you can find Queer Studies and Queer Theory courses at many colleges. The word queer is used in this book in a positive and affirming way. Queer is simply "other than the expected or average," which is straight. Some people believe the labels gay, lesbian, bisexual, or transgender are too limiting, so queer is also a great word because it frees you from using a specific label if you don't want to. It's your life. How you identify is a very personal decision and one that only you can make.

The glossary (page 200) includes the GLBTQ terms used in this book, along with words you might come across elsewhere. For now, let's look at the basics.

G is for gay. This term often is used to describe both homosexual men and lesbians. As it refers to men, gay describes men who are physically and emotionally attracted to other men. The word *gay* didn't come into wide use to describe homosexual people until around the 1950s.

L is for lesbian. Lesbians are women who are physically and emotionally attracted to other women. The word *lesbian* has its origins with the Greek poet Sappho, who was born sometime between 630 and 612 BC For part of her life, Sappho lived on the island of Lesbos. Many of her poems dealt with same-sex love between women, and as a result, the island's name became synonymous with homosexual women. That's how the term lesbian was born.

B is for bisexual. Bisexual people can be emotionally and physically attracted to people of either sex. Sometimes people refer to themselves as bisexual as a means of identifying themselves as questioning, or they identify as bisexual and then later identify as gay or lesbian. However, many bisexual people are bisexual, period, and that is what they will remain.

Bisexuality is one of the least understood expressions of sexuality. Unfortunately, people who identify as bisexual can face ignorance even from the gay community. They might be told they "just can't admit they're gay" or "can't make up their minds." Bisexuality has been scientifically proven to be a valid identity (read about the Kinsey Scale on page 10). As with all others, bisexual people should be accepted for who they are.

T is for transgender. Transgender people have feelings of being a different gender from their physical anatomies. What it means to be transgender is complicated and often misunderstood. One misconception is that all transgender people want to have surgery and/or take hormones to change their bodies. Some do, others don't. Another misconception is that all trans people are homosexual. Transgender people are often straight, but just like everyone else, they can be gay, lesbian, or bisexual. Some trans people start out identifying as gay, lesbian, or bisexual, then later realize they are transgender.

Some of the issues and emotions transgender people may face are similar to those that gay, lesbian, and bisexual people often experience. Feelings of isolation and the desire to come out, for example, are experiences that all GLBTQ people may have. However, there are other feelings and considerations that can come with identifying as the opposite physical gender (or not identifying as either gender). Some of these issues are addressed in Chapter 10 (page 167).

Q is for questioning. People who are questioning are uncertain of their sexual orientations or gender identities, or they may just prefer not to label themselves with any particular orientation. Many teens are starting to embrace identifying themselves as questioning. A lot of things are changing during adolescence, and deciding that you're questioning can remove the pressure of having to choose a label like gay, lesbian, bisexual, or straight right away.

A Biology Lesson? The Science of GLBTQ

Why are some people GLBTQ and others aren't? At this point, there isn't a definitive answer. Scientists, philosophers, psychologists, and a host of others have offered opinions and theories to answer the question, but for now, there isn't a 100 percent proof-positive reason. There has, however, been a lot of research attempting to determine what makes people GLBTQ. Thanks to these efforts, scientists, healthcare professionals, and the general public have access to expanded information on sexual orientation and gender identity.

The Kinsey Report

In the 1940s, a scientist named Dr. Alfred Kinsey and his team of researchers conducted a study of human sexuality in men. Based on this research, Kinsey determined that most men are neither completely gay nor completely straight. Instead, while some are at either end of the spectrum, most fall somewhere in the middle. He developed a six-point scale—the Kinsey Scale—to illustrate this spectrum.

The Kinsey Scale was revolutionary not only because it looked at queerness as predetermined, but also because it showed a vast gray area between GLBTQ and straight. Before Kinsey, many experts thought it was black and white—straight people were 100 percent straight and queer people were 100 percent queer. Many also thought that straight people were "normal" and "well-adjusted," while queer people were "sick" or "deviant." Kinsey's research helped dispel this myth and showed that homosexuality and bisexuality were much more common than previously thought.

Kinsey was so intrigued by his research on male sexuality that he expanded his later work to include women, too. His best-known publications were the books *Sexual Behavior in the Human Male* (1948) and *Sexual Behavior in the Human Female* (1953).

Though the statistical methods Kinsey used to conduct his studies fall short of the standards used for research today, there is strong evidence that people fall on a continuum of sexuality. While some people show up on points 6 or 0, most fall at one of the numbers in between.

If you've never thought of sexuality on a spectrum, the idea can be confusing. But if you think about all of the complex factors that contribute to making a single human being, it can begin to make more sense. Every human characteristic is on a spectrum. Even within a single quality, there can be great variety. Take eye color, for example. A person with blue eyes can have light blue eyes, deep blue eyes, or blue-gray eyes. Being human means being varied.

Maybe you're attracted exclusively to either girls or guys. Maybe you're usually attracted to boys, but there's something about that girl in your chemistry class that really intrigues you. Or maybe at the last football game you spent just as much time looking at the cheerleaders as the players. All of these responses are natural.

Sexual Orientation: The Kinsey Scale

0 Exclusively heterosexual

1 Predominantly heterosexual, only incidentally homosexual

2 Predominantly heterosexual, but more than incidentally homosexual

3 Equally heterosexual and homosexual

4 Predominantly homosexual, but more than incidentally heterosexual

5 Predominantly homosexual, only incidentally heterosexual

6 Exclusively homosexual

BEEN THERE

"For me, there was a lot of uncertainty in high school. I liked half the guys in my senior class, but I also had a crush on two girls on my block. That's very confusing at an age when you are changing physically and mentally." —Enrique, 20

Why Are People Queer or Straight?

That's the million-dollar question. Over the course of your life, you'll hear a lot of theories about why some people are GLBTQ and others aren't. There are queer people who believe you can choose to be GLBTQ. There are straight people who believe you can't. Some say it's like putting on a suit that you can take off at any time. Others believe that it's something deep inside you. You might even hear someone talk about how an experience "made" someone gay. Lots of people have their own theories about it, and if you haven't already, you might develop one of your own. You might also decide that you don't care "why."

While some scientists are working to uncover a genetic component that makes people queer, most mental health professionals and GLBTQ advocates believe that being GLBTQ is most likely the result of a complex interaction of environmental and biological factors. The American Psychiatric Association and advocacy groups like PFLAG don't believe that being queer is a choice. The American Psychological Association maintains unequivocally that "human beings cannot choose to be either gay or straight." In its pamphlet "Answers to Your Questions for a Better Understanding of Sexual Orientation & Homosexuality" it states, "No findings have emerged that permit scientists to conclude that sexual orientation is determined by any particular factor or factors. . . . Most people experience little or no sense of choice about their sexual orientation."

Wanting to Change and People Who Want to Change You

Coming to terms with being GLBTQ involves many stages. Early in that process, many teens wish they could change. Some ignore how they feel and try to act as if they're straight—going on dates, having romantic relationships, and sometimes even having sex.

Many of the people who have gone on to become leaders in the GLBTQ community started out just as confused and scared as you might be. Transgender activist and writer Kate Bornstein, who was born with male anatomy but always felt like a female, writes in her book *Gender Outlaw: On Men, Women, and the Rest of Us* about her experience of trying to hide her feelings of being a girl. "I knew from age four on that something was wrong with me being a guy, and I spent most of my life avoiding the issue," she writes. "I hid out in textbooks, pulp fiction, and drugs and alcohol. I buried my head in the sands of television, college, a lot of lovers, and three marriages." Bornstein eventually stopped trying to hide and grew to accept and love her true identity.

Similarly, Ellen DeGeneres has spoken openly about her reluctance to come out because of her intense fear of rejection. After her very public coming out in 1997, Ellen's career did falter for a period of time. Now, however, she has risen to become one of the most beloved figures on daytime television. *The Ellen DeGeneres Show* won nearly 30 Daytime Emmy Awards in its first six seasons.

Overwhelmingly, mainstream medical and professional organizations maintain that there is nothing wrong with being queer and that no one should attempt a "cure." In fact, the American Academy of Pediatrics, the American Counseling Association, the American Psychiatric Association, the National Association of School Psychologists, and the National Association of Social Workers all maintain that queerness is *not* a mental disorder.

In its publication "Answers to Your Questions for a Better Understanding of Sexual Orientation & Homosexuality," the American Psychological Association states, "Both heterosexual behavior and homosexual behavior are normal aspects of human sexuality. . . . Despite the persistence of stereotypes that portray lesbian, gay, and bisexual people as disturbed, several decades of mental health research and clinical experience have led all mainstream medical and mental health organizations in this country to conclude that these orientations represent normal forms of human experience."

However, some people believe you can change your gender identity or sexual orientation through therapy or other means. So-called "reparative therapy" or "transformational ministries" try to change or "cure" GLBTQ people. Reparative therapy, which is sometimes called "conversion therapy," involves psychotherapy aimed at eliminating feelings of homosexuality. Transformational ministries use religion to try to change people. Groups like Exodus International try to "free" people from being queer by pointing them toward God. (For more information on aspects of religion and homosexuality, see Chapter 9 beginning on page 150.)

Reparative therapy and transformational ministries can be very destructive to queer people's self-esteem because the goal is to convince those who are GLBTQ that their thoughts and feelings are wrong and unnatural. If you need help coming to terms with being GLBTQ, or if you just want someone to talk to, seeking therapy or counseling to discuss these issues is a good idea. But talk to someone who won't try to make you feel like it's wrong to be who you are. You don't need to try to fix who you are, because nothing is wrong with you in the first place.

The National Gay and Lesbian Task Force Policy Institute published a report called "Youth in the Crosshairs: The Third Wave of Ex-Gay Activism." The report details efforts by specific organizations to target GLBTQ teens and concludes, "There is a growing body of evidence that conversion therapy not only does not work, but also can be extremely harmful, resulting in depression, social isolation from family and friends, low self-esteem, internalized homophobia, and even attempted suicide." Further, "Many conversion therapy clients were not informed about alternative treatment options, including therapy that could have helped them accept their sexual orientation." The American Psychiatric Association has condemned reparative therapies, stating that attempts to transform gay or bisexual people into heterosexual people are pointless and often motivated by personal prejudices.

BEEN THERE

"When I first started to understand myself and tried to accept who I was, I was devastated. I remember a day when I took out my student Bible and searched for hours on homosexuality. When I finally found it, I was sobbing so hard I could barely breathe. There were a couple of passages that I thought were scolding me. They told me I was evil and hateful, that my kind is unforgiven and will forever burn. It was the harshest thing I had ever read. I probably prayed more within that week than I had ever prayed in my life. I begged for God to tell me if I was wrong and evil. I cried to myself, trying to get myself to believe that I'm not what they say I am. It took me a while to pull through that." —Sonia, 19

Your Personal Geography: Exploring Who You Are

What it all boils down to is that it doesn't really matter what the "experts" say. The only person who is a true expert when it comes to you is you, so what matters is what *you* say. You're the only person who can make a definitive statement about who you are—or you can decide not to make a definitive statement. While you can't control whether you're GLBTQ, you can shape how you feel about yourself. You have the power to improve your self-esteem.

Yes, No, Maybe So: It's Okay to Be Questioning

Even if few people talk about it, questioning your sexual orientation is more common than you might think. Cornell University professor Ritch Savin-Williams is a well-known authority on issues surrounding GLBTQ teens. In his book *The New Gay Teenager,* Savin-Williams asserts that, based on his own study of teens, "it is safe to conclude that at least 15 percent and maybe as high as 20 percent of all adolescents have some degree of a same-sex orientation." He adds, "Less than half of these individuals are exclusively or near exclusively same-sex oriented." Therefore, teens who have same-sex attractions far outnumber the estimated three to four percent who self-identify as gay or bisexual or who report having engaged in same-sex sexual activity.

What's the Rush?

According to Caitlin Ryan and Donna Futterman—two of the first researchers to broadly address issues of GLBTQ teens—many gay and lesbian young people begin to self-identify around age 16. Their first awareness of homosexual attraction, though, likely occurred around age 9 for males and age 10 for females. Children start to become aware of biological differences between boys and girls at around age three. Transgender people often report feeling conflict between their physical anatomy and gender identity throughout childhood and adolescence. The point is, for most GLBTQ young people, developing an understanding of sexuality is a long process.

BEEN THERE

"I realized I was GLBTQ when I was young, like 11 or 12. I always had an interest in the female sex, ever since I can remember. I distinctly remember watching television and 'liking' a pretty woman on the screen and wanting to touch her. I thought it was normal and didn't really think anything of it until I was 16 and I finally came out to myself." —Elena, 20

"It's hard to say definitively how I became aware of my gender identity. I think it was really while I was surfing websites and reading stories about transgender people. It was then that I realized not all guys had dreams of suddenly and inexplicably being changed into a girl." —Chris, 19

"I think I've known all my life that I am bisexual, even though I didn't always have a word for it. I can remember playing with another little girl when I was young, seven or eight maybe, and we'd play 'boyfriend' and 'girlfriend.' I have always been attracted to boys and girls, but it wasn't until a friend of mine came out and told me he was gay that I started thinking that I was bisexual." —June, 19

Common Feelings When You're Awakening

Although everyone reacts differently to the idea that they might be GLBTQ, people usually experience a very common progression of stages. Some go through this process more quickly than others, and many people spend a lot more time in one stage than another. Sociologist Richard Troiden described the process in the *Journal of Homosexuality*:

Stage One: Sensitization. Feelings of being different from others in a fundamental way can begin well before puberty. This is usually a very challenging time that can make people feel isolated from family and friends.

Stage Two: Identity confusion. People start becoming more aware of actual same-sex thoughts and feelings. During this stage, learned negative thoughts about homosexuality can cause individuals to feel betrayed by their own thoughts and feelings.

Stage Three: Identity assumption. Things get better at this point in the process. It's typically when people begin to find more positive, accurate information about what it means to be GLBTQ and start to identify that way.

Stage Four: Commitment. Historically, people often didn't reach this stage until adulthood; today, more teens are reaching it at progressively younger ages. This is likely the result of more positive portrayals of GLBTQ people in the media and broader access to accurate information about what it means to be GLBTQ. During this stage, people incorporate sexual identity into all aspects of their lives—a big part of which is "coming out" to other people as GLBTQ. (See Chapter 3, page 48, for more information on coming out.)

BEEN THERE

"I came out to my sister and she was very weird about it, but things are becoming easier as I get older. I'm just becoming more comfortable with being bisexual." —Charlotte, 19

▼ Art Imitates Life The character Kurt on the television network show *Glee* is a good example of a young person who has progressed to the last stage of the awakening process. In an early episode, Kurt comes out to the character Mercedes—another singer in the glee club—to explain why he can't reciprocate her crush on him. As the series continues, viewers see Kurt develop a more active acceptance of himself as gay, which he demonstrates by becoming more open with others about who he is.

In real life, Chris Colfer, the actor who plays Kurt, has spoken about his own reluctance to be open about his identity when he was in high school. Colfer has said that many of his own experiences informed not only how he plays Kurt on *Glee*, but also some of the storylines on the show. **▼**

Myths, Generalizations, and Just Plain Absurd Ideas About GLBTQ People . . . and the Truth

At school, many classmates might follow stereotypes. Based on how people dress or what they like to do after class, individuals may get pigeonholed into categories such as jock, geek, player, slacker, baller, goody-goody, and so on. You've probably noticed that the problem with these labels is that they're one-dimensional and don't fully describe a person. You could dress like an athlete but have the soul of an artist, and vice versa.

The more you get to know someone, the less appropriate labels seem. For example, try describing your closest friend in a one-word stereotype. You'll probably find that a single word just doesn't do him or her justice.

GLBTQ people are especially susceptible to stereotyping. One reason is that some individuals are afraid to challenge these stereotypes because they fear others might assume they're GLBTQ and start to harass them. Another reason stereotypes are strong is the lack of positive and accurate portrayals of GLBTQ people in the media. Although more are present now, they still aren't abundant.

Also, many GLBTQ people are afraid to come out because they fear rejection or even physical harm. The lack of an accepting environment keeps some individuals in hiding, which allows misinformation to thrive.

Fortunately, things are improving. Activists have helped change how GLBTQ people are viewed in society. And the media is showing more GLBTQ people as everyday people, including in shows such as *Glee, Ugly Betty, The Ellen DeGeneres Show, Modern Family,* and *Grey's Anatomy.* There is even an all-queer television network called Logo.

Still, ignorance persists. For example, take the following GLBTQ stereotypes. You might have heard some—or even all—of these misguided ideas or statements. And don't think it's just straight people who say these things. Unfortunately, stereotyping exists within the GLBTQ community, too.

15 Absolutely Ridiculous Queer Stereotypes (and the Truth)

Myth #1: GLBTQ people are unhappy being who they are.

The truth: For a long time, society has painted a picture of GLBTQ people as living secretive or tormented lives. But a lot of queer people live open and happy lives with loving families, just like straight people. The reality is that GLBTQ people can encounter difficulties for being what many in society view as "different." This is not related to what it means to be queer. Rather, a lack of understanding among others can cause challenges for GLBTQ people. And being straight doesn't guarantee a life free of difficulties. For both GLBTQ and straight people, how we deal with life's challenges helps determine our happiness and success.

Myth #2: Gay men are attracted to all men, lesbians are attracted to all women, and bisexuals are attracted to just plain everyone.

The truth: Just like straight people, queer people have personal tastes in what they like, whether it's food, cars, or people they're attracted to. Because the stereotype is so common, some people may be uncomfortable when they first meet a GLBTQ person. ("Oh, he's gay. . . . He must be checking me out.") But coming *out* to someone is not the same thing as coming *on* to the person. The more people are exposed to gays, lesbians, and bisexuals, the more they come to understand that.

Myth #3: Gay men want to be women and lesbians want to be men.

The truth: Being transgender and being gay or lesbian are very different things. Some people have such a hard time understanding same-sex attractions that they assume that gay men and women actually want to be the opposite physical sex. This stereotype also has roots in how some gay men and lesbians challenge gender norms when expressing themselves. Gay men who are seen as more *femme* (a term used to describe both males and females who act and dress in stereotypically feminine ways) and lesbians who dress or act more *butch* (a term used to describe both males and females who act and dress in stereotypically masculine ways) are often assumed to want to change their genders. A related myth is that butch lesbians and femme gay men just want to draw attention to themselves. The reality is that the way femme guys and butch girls present themselves is simply a form of expression in the same way that anyone's—gay or straight—personality or style of dressing is a representation of who they are. When we start criticizing anyone's right to dress or be who they want to be, we start suppressing all of our rights to do so.

Myth #4: Gay men hate women and lesbians hate men.

The truth: Being gay means you are physically and emotionally attracted to people of the same sex. It has nothing to do with a hatred for people of the opposite gender. For example, women aren't driven to be gay because they hate or had bad experiences with men. Lesbians want to form physical and/or love relationships with women because of a deep desire to be with women, and gay men want to form physical and/or love relationships because of a deep desire to be with men.

Myth #5: Queer people "flaunt it."

The truth: GLBTQ people who have bumper stickers on their cars, get involved in the queer civil rights movement, or hold hands in public are sometimes accused of "flaunting it." Some straight people wonder why queer people don't just keep it to themselves—stay invisible. However, in a society where the assumption is that people are straight, GLBTQ people often feel the need to challenge that assumption or self-identify to let other GLBTQ people know they're not alone. Sometimes people make their orientations known as a means of standing up for themselves, or simply as a gesture to remind others that not everyone is straight.

Additionally, straight people who hold hands in public are rarely accused of flaunting being straight. Most GLBTQ people simply desire the same freedom of expression of love for their boyfriend, girlfriend, spouse, or significant other. Often they're not trying to make any political or social statements, they're just being themselves.

▼ **Queers in the Military** GLBTQ people are highly decorated soldiers, sailors, airmen, and Marines, who can now serve openly. The debate over the federal "Don't Ask, Don't Tell" (DADT) policy—which forbid openly gay people from serving in the U.S. military—was officially repealed by President Obama on December 22, 2010. In the preceding months and weeks, the debate over DADT had grown in intensity with the ongoing conflicts in Iraq and Afghanistan.

In 2009, President Obama pledged to end DADT. In 2010, Defense Secretary Robert Gates severely limited how it could be enforced. Most senior military leaders, including the highest ranking military officer in the nation—Admiral Mike Mullen, the chairman of the Joint Chiefs of Staff—voiced support for repeal of the policy. However, strong opposition remained among some in the Senate and the military. As a result, the military conducted one of the largest surveys in the history of the armed forces, asking service members and their families their feelings about the potential repeal of the policy. The survey committee also interviewed current and former gay and lesbian service members, including many who had been "separated" from the military under DADT. The committee's report, issued November 30, 2010, stated, "The results . . . reveal a widespread attitude among a solid majority of service members that repeal of Don't Ask, Don't Tell will not have a negative impact on their ability to conduct their military mission."

After an intense series of debates, the Senate and House voted to overturn the policy. It is now up to the military to implement full integration of people who are openly gay or lesbian in the armed services. While this process will take time and will likely hit some bumps, the repeal of DADT is a huge step forward in the GLBTQ civil rights movement and a landmark in American history. ▼

Myth #6: Bisexual people are gay men and lesbians in denial.

The truth: Unfortunately, bisexuals are sometimes discriminated against by both straight and queer people. This is due to a common lack of understanding about the validity of bisexuality as a permanent sexual and emotional orientation. Bisexual people are just that—people—and they deserve to have their feelings respected just like everyone else, queer or straight. While it's true that some people identify as bisexual for a time before realizing they are gay or lesbian (or even transgender), many people are bisexual, period.

Myth #7: Transgender people are all drag queens and drag kings.

The truth: Drag queens are men who dress as women and perform for entertainment and drag kings are women who dress as men and perform for entertainment. Transgender people have a deep, personal identification with a gender that is different from their anatomy. Transgender people don't dress or act certain ways to get attention or for entertainment, but instead to reflect who they are inside. Some transgender people are also drag queens or drag kings, but most are not.

Myth #8: GLBTQ people are all into partying and drugs.

The truth: For a long time, some of the only safe places for GLBTQ people to get together were in queer or queer-friendly bars and clubs. They became not only places to socialize, but also, in some cases, places to meet and organize civil rights efforts. The club and bar scenes are still popular today, but GLBTQ people socialize in other places, as well. Unfortunately, many media portrayals of GLBTQ people are limited to sensational and racy depictions of the queer party scene. Even worse, those are the only images some straight people have been exposed to. Just like straight people, though, queer people have interests that go well beyond partying. And plenty of queer people don't "do the scene" at all.

Myth #9: Queer people recruit.

The truth: This myth is rooted in a misunderstanding that GLBTQ people choose to be who they are, and so therefore they can talk or turn someone else into being queer. An especially vicious aspect of this myth is the accusation that GLBTQ people "recruit" young people. In fact, this book has been banned from a few libraries because some people allege that the information in it is designed to "turn" young people GLBTQ. Being gay isn't like buying a car—a skilled salesperson can't just talk you into it. Personal identity and attraction are highly individual and can't be dictated by someone else.

What is true is that after being exposed to or spending time with GLBTQ people, a person might realize that he or she has similar personal feelings or characteristics. Many queer people recall understanding themselves better after meeting, reading about, or listening to others who are GLBTQ.

BEEN THERE

"In college, I started spending a lot of time with a friend who was a lesbian. I didn't understand why, but I felt really compelled to hang out with her almost all the time. When I came out, my mom accused my friend of turning me gay. But it wasn't that. It was that spending time with her and having her put words to what I had been feeling for years made me realize I was like her all along." — Jasmine, 22

Myth #10: Gay men are interior decorators, fashion designers, and hairdressers, and lesbians are construction workers, police officers, and social workers.
The truth: Some of us are, and that's great, but many of us aren't. Look at fashion model Jenny Shimizu, who is a lesbian, and Mark Bingham, a gay rugby player who acted with great bravery to help bring down Flight 93 before it could hit the U.S. Capitol on September 11, 2001. From supermodels to heroes, we are everywhere.

Myth #11: Queer people can't be parents.
The truth: Many queer people have children, and same-sex parenting is becoming more common. Some GLBTQ people adopt, while others have children from previous straight marriages. Still others undergo artificial insemination or use a surrogate mother. It used to be that a "normal" family was nuclear—a mom, a dad, and two kids. Today, there might be two moms, two dads, a mom and two dads, and so on. More states are allowing second-parent adoption in same-sex households and are permitting gay couples to be foster parents. In the generations to come, more people will have gay parents, which should lead to a broader understanding and acceptance of GLBTQ people.

Myth #12: GLBTQ people only live in urban areas.

The truth: There's a bumper sticker that reads, "We're everywhere." That's no joke. Commonly accepted estimates suggest that as many as 1 in 10 people are GLBTQ. Being queer isn't dictated by where you live or how you grow up. It's likely that GLBTQ people are more visible in urban areas because there is greater acceptance of differences there (although some rural areas are very accepting). It's easy to feel alone when you first realize you're queer, but you aren't.

Find Support
YouthResource (www.amplifyyourvoice.org/YouthResource). This website, written by and for teens, features resources and advice for young GLBTQ people (including those in rural areas). The site also features information on advocacy efforts you can join.

ACLU Youth & Schools (www.aclu.org/lgbt-rights/youth-schools). The American Civil Liberties Union (ACLU) advocates for equality for all people. Visit this site for tools that can be helpful for promoting tolerance in schools, including those in rural areas.

Myth #13: Gay men can't commit to a long-term relationship, and lesbians can't *not* commit.

The truth: The stereotype that gay men can't be monogamous and lesbians can't be single is persistent. Much of this is based more on stereotypes about gender in general than about GLBTQ men and women. Men have gotten the reputation for being unable to commit, and women are often thought of as always wanting to settle down. The truth is, these are just generalizations, and there are many happy gay male couples and plenty of single lesbians.

Myth #14: GLBTQ people are "immoral."

The truth: Some misinformed people view GLBTQ people as immoral or deviant. Being queer relates to one's personal sexual orientation; being immoral is a subjective assessment or judgment based on how someone views someone else's behavior. Everyone has a different view of what is moral or immoral, and a lot goes into making up these personal opinions. What's important is that GLBTQ teens understand that someone's personal judgment is not fact.

Myth #15: GLBTQ people are not religious or spiritual.
The truth: This is closely related to Myth #14. Many queers do participate in organized religion or abide by a set of personally held spiritual beliefs. And many churches, temples, and other places of worship welcome and accept GLBTQ people. Some churches—the Metropolitan Community Church being one of the best known—take a strong stand on human rights, including GLBTQ civil rights.

Many churches have been divided over whether or not to welcome GLBTQ congregants and/or allow queer people to serve as religious officials. One of the most publicized instances has been in the Lutheran church. In August 2009, the Evangelical Lutheran Church voted to allow gay, lesbian, bisexual, and transgender people to openly serve as pastors. Further, the church voted that GLBTQ pastors would not have to be celibate and they could live openly with regard to their personal relationships. On July 25, 2010, the church officially welcomed the first seven GLBTQ pastors into its ranks—a successful ending to a decades-long struggle.

For more information on GLBTQ people and issues of religion and spirituality, including examples from other religions and denominations, see Chapter 9 (page 150).

Your Own Beliefs About GLBTQ People

Some of the most difficult GLBTQ stereotypes to conquer can be the ones you hold yourself. You might not realize it, but even you could believe some inaccurate information about GLBTQ people. By adolescence, most teens have internalized at least some negative messages they've received.

Stereotypes about GLBTQ people can also make it tough to know that you're queer. Some people say they had trouble figuring out that they are GLBTQ because they didn't seem to fit the "definition" of what that meant. But it turns out that definition was based on stereotypes, and what it means to be GLBTQ is different for each person.

Out comedian Elvira Kurt has a bit in her stand-up routine when she comes out to the audience, then teases some of them about their shocked reactions. "Well, she has short hair, but she's wearing a dress and lipstick. Is she butch or femme?" she jokes.

She then explains that she's part of a vast space between butch and femme that she likes to call "fellagirly."

Some GLBTQ people adhere to some of the same stereotypes about queer people that many straight people do. Maybe you think that because you're GLBTQ, you won't be able to pursue your chosen profession or have children. Maybe you think it means you'll have to dress or act a certain way. But that's not true. Contrary to popular belief, there isn't a "gay lifestyle." Whatever it means to be GLBTQ is really about what it means to you, not to anyone else. The GLBTQ community is as rich and diverse as the straight community, and there's plenty of room for you just as you are.

Check Your Head

It can be difficult to face negative stereotypes, especially when you apply them to yourself. Here are some thoughts to help you unlearn some of the negative misinformation that could be affecting how you feel about yourself. If you're struggling, repeat them to yourself. The more you do, the more you can start to believe them.

1. I am a human being who happens to be (or might be) queer. It isn't all that I am, but it's a part of me and a part that I embrace.
2. Being GLBTQ means only that—it's my sexual orientation/gender identity. I can be anything I want to be.
3. I am my own person. I can wear what I want, say what I want, and do what I want.

Chapter 2

Homophobia

Hate is not a family value.

Even though we know there have been GLBTQ people since the beginning of time, many history books largely ignore queer individuals. When GLBTQ people are acknowledged, they are sometimes portrayed as immoral or unnatural. This combination of invisibility and misinformation has contributed to widespread ignorance regarding GLBTQ people. That ignorance often reveals itself as *homophobia*.

Homophobia can put a lot of pressure on you, especially at school. You may be comfortable with being GLBTQ, but classmates, teachers, and even friends might be pretty *un*comfortable with it. Some people may even be hateful or violent.

BEEN THERE
"I'm like everyone else. I'm still human and I still have feelings. The hard part is when ignorant people say you choose to be this way and that it's your fault and it's wrong. It makes you feel like a target."
—Shannon, 20

Homophobia can make you feel terrible—all you want to do is be yourself, but no one wants to let you. It can also inspire you to try changing the world. Either way, the absolute most important thing to remember is that *homophobia is not about you*. It's about other people and their ignorance. It's not based on who you really are, but on misconceptions and untruths. Homophobia might cause you problems in life, but it's not *your* problem. You didn't do anything to bring it on or to deserve it.

So where does homophobia come from, and if there's nothing wrong with GLBTQ people, why doesn't it just go away?

The 411 on Hate: The Roots of Homophobia

Homophobia is a negative emotion like fear, anger, or suspicion—or a combination of these—toward someone for being GLBTQ. It is rooted in ignorance about GLBTQ people. Homophobia can be overt, like someone shouting "dyke!" or "fag!" in the hall. It can also be subtle, like a teammate quietly avoiding being near you in the locker room.

From Uncomfortable to Hateful: Shades of Homophobia

Although homophobia is never a good thing, it has degrees ranging from mild to severe. People who are ignorant about what it means to be GLBTQ *can* change their negative ideas when they find out a friend or family member is queer. They begin to understand that we are human beings just like everyone else.

For others, homophobia is more deeply rooted and takes form as hatred of GLBTQ people. These individuals may act out in ways that range from lobbying for anti-queer legislation to bullying and physically hurting GLBTQ people. A lot of homophobic people would never dream of physically hurting another human being. But heartbreaking incidents like Matthew Shepard's brutal murder in 1998 and widespread occurrences of queer young people committing suicide because of anti-GLBTQ bullying show that a lot of hatred still exists in this world. Such incidents mean that queer people need to think seriously about their safety.

What Makes People Homophobic?

The dictionary defines a phobia as an irrational fear. So, by definition, homophobia is not based on reason.

According to clinical psychologist Dr. Sandy Loiterstein, who has worked as a support group coordinator for the Washington, D.C., chapter of Parents, Families and Friends of Lesbians and Gays (PFLAG), homophobia can have a variety of sources. "One of these is the perception that being GLBTQ is a choice," she said in an interview. "Some people get very angry or frustrated with GLBTQ people because they don't understand why they would make such a choice. There's also an inability to see GLBTQ people as individuals. Instead, they're seen through stereotypes. Ancient fears of differentness, probably the major source of homophobia, have been perpetuated by religious and other institutions, including mental health organizations. As recently as 1976, the American Psychiatric Association finally removed their classification of homosexuality as a mental illness."

In some cases, the historic roots of anti-GLBTQ attitudes don't have much to do with homosexuality. In some cultures, any sexual contact between two people that could not result in the conception of a child (such as oral sex) was considered sinful or morally wrong regardless of whether it was between people of different sexes or the same one. In some cases, it was the act rather than the biological sex of the people engaged in it that was frowned upon. According to *Hidden from History: Reclaiming the Gay & Lesbian Past,* some historians believe that in certain cultures and religions the roots of homophobia extend back to such beliefs.

For more information on common fears and myths about GLBTQ people, see page 18 in Chapter 1.

GLBTQ People Can Be Homophobic, Too

Another kind of homophobia is *internalized homophobia*. People with internalized homophobia have difficulty accepting that they are GLBTQ. They feel guilty about who they are or believe that being queer means something is wrong with them.

George Weinberg, the psychologist and GLBTQ rights activist who coined the terms *homophobia* and *internalized homophobia,* stated in a 2002 interview in the magazine *Gay Today* that internalized homophobia is the fear of being different, singled out, punished, or laughed at. Weinberg explained that internalized homophobia decreases as people are able to accept themselves for who they are, regardless of what others might think.

Invisibility as Homophobia

When you're GLBTQ, sometimes you wish people would just stop acting like it's a huge deal. Conversely, there are situations when queer people might seem nonexistent. For example, if you're a guy, it can be frustrating, embarrassing, or nerve-racking when relatives or others continually ask, "Do you have a girlfriend yet?" instead of asking something that makes fewer assumptions, like, "Are you dating anyone special?"

Negative Images of GLBTQ People in Movies

Hollywood has long been famous for playing on people's fears of GLBTQ people. In *The Celluloid Closet: Homosexuality in the Movies,* Vito Russo explores the history of GLBTQ people in film. He discusses how the portrayal of GLBTQ people in Hollywood films has run the gamut from invisibility (nope, no queers here) to homophobic stereotypes (queer people are silly or scary). From sissies to psychotic killers, you may be surprised at how long certain negative stereotypes about queer people, that still exist in films today, have been around.

Questions that assume you're straight are good examples of *heterosexism*. Heterosexism is the idea that heterosexual people are the norm and that GLBTQ people are somehow abnormal. The assumption that all people are heterosexual or that only heterosexuality is "normal" contributes to homophobia. The disparate marriage rights for homosexual couples and heterosexual couples in the United States are an example of heterosexism.

The Big Bad World?
Homophobia in Society and at School

Have you ever heard of *mob mentality*? It's when an individual might not normally do something, but because she sees other people doing it, she thinks it must be okay or feels pressure to join in.

One reason homophobia is so common is mob mentality. Mob mentality often plays a role when people gang up on GLBTQ teens and bully them, including in person or online. When a handful of people speak out strongly against GLBTQ people and their ideas go unchallenged, ignorance and hatred can persist.

How common is homophobia? Common enough that GLBTQ activists are fighting against it all over the world. In the United States, the Gay and Lesbian Alliance Against Defamation (GLAAD) is working to encourage positive, informed portrayals of GLBTQ people in the media. The Human Rights Campaign (HRC) and National Gay and Lesbian Task Force (NGLTF) are working to enact social change by getting legislation passed that protects GLBTQ people and their civil rights. Internationally, PFLAG is working to increase understanding of and support for GLBTQ people by changing attitudes about them. These are just some of the many groups working to make the world a better place for GLBTQ people.

▼ **Marriage Rights in Other Countries** On July 20, 2005, Canada became the first country in the Americas to recognize same-sex marriage. Other countries with same-sex marriage rights or civil partnerships include Belgium, Croatia, the Czech Republic, Denmark, Finland, France, Germany, Hungary, Iceland, Ireland, Luxembourg, Mexico, the Netherlands, New Zealand, Norway, Portugal, Slovenia, South Africa, Spain, Sweden, Switzerland, and the United Kingdom. ▼

Every day people are lobbying legislators to pass queer-friendly laws such as the Employment Non-Discrimination Act (ENDA), which would prohibit workplace discrimination based on sexual orientation or gender identity. California's Student Safety and Violence Prevention Act states that all California schools have a duty to protect students from discrimination and/or harassment on the basis of sexual orientation or gender identity. In 2002, student George Loomis, along with a coalition of local groups, PFLAG, the American Civil Liberties Union (ACLU), and the Gay-Straight Alliance Network (GSA Network) used the law as a basis for a successful lawsuit against Loomis's school district for failing to take actions to protect him from harassment.

In 2009, 14-year-old Jacob Sullivan, with the help of the New York Civil Liberties Union, filed suit against the Mohawk Central School District on the grounds that the school district allegedly failed to protect Jacob against ongoing and relentless harassment, physical abuse, and threats of violence based on Jacob's sexual orientation and nonconformity with masculine stereotypes. "People always make fun of what they don't understand, but the school has a responsibility to protect people," Jacob is quoted as saying in an interview. "I shouldn't have to fear for my safety at school. No one should." On March 29, 2010, the court reached a settlement that awarded Jacob $50,000 from the school district. The school district also was required to pay $25,000 in legal fees to the New York Civil Liberties Union and to pay for professional counseling for Jacob.

The National Safe Schools Improvement Act, introduced in the 111th Congress and in the Senate in August 2010, would amend the Safe and Drug-Free Schools and Communities Act (part of the No Child Left Behind Act) to require schools and districts receiving federal funds to adopt codes of conduct that specifically prohibit bullying and harassment, including on the basis of sexual orientation or gender identity. The Act would also require states to report data on bullying and harassment to the Department of Education.

Homophobia in the Hallways:
Bullying and Harassment at School

If you've ever been singled out verbally or physically because you're GLBTQ (or perceived to be), you're not alone. According to the "2009 National School Climate Survey" conducted by the Gay, Lesbian and Straight Education Network (GLSEN), nearly 60 percent of students reported feeling unsafe at school because of their sexual orientation, and more than a third felt unsafe because of their gender identity or gender expression. In addition, 40 percent of GLBTQ students surveyed reported experiencing physical harassment (such as being blocked from walking down the hall), and nearly 19 percent reported being physically assaulted (punched, kicked, etc.) at school in the last year because of their sexual orientation.

The anti-GLBTQ bullying epidemic came to national attention in the fall of 2010 after a series of young gay people committed suicide. In many cases, they had been victims of anti-queer bullying. One of the most publicized deaths was that of Tyler Clementi, a Rutgers University freshman whose roommate posted a video of him in an intimate encounter with another male and sent messages encouraging others to watch. Clementi committed suicide after finding out what his roommate had done. His death drew attention to the skyrocketing rates of bullying and harassment occurring in schools.

> ### Find Legislative Updates
> **Human Rights Campaign (www.hrc.org).** For updates on the status of bills currently under debate and more information about GLBTQ-related legislation, visit the HRC website. You'll discover that the legislation discussed in this book is just the tip of the iceberg. Many more GLBTQ-rights bills are being considered at the state and federal levels.

BEEN THERE
"When I was in the 11th grade and being harassed constantly, the teacher did nothing. I think that she should have." —Brian, 19

Legislators, parents, educators, and various activists continue to debate about whether to provide young people with access to information about GLBTQ people. Advocates suggest that giving students positive and accurate information about GLBTQ issues will reduce bullying and harassment of those who are or who are perceived to be GLBTQ. Opponents claim that these efforts encourage and promote queerness. This belief hearkens back to one of the commonly held myths about GLBTQ people—that we "recruit." (See page 18 for a list of myths—and the truth—about GLBTQ people.)

Many groups, including GLSEN and PFLAG, have "safe schools" movements where adults and teens work together to make school environments safer for young people who are or who are perceived to be GLBTQ. Often these groups work to institute anti-bullying policies that include harassment based on sexual orientation, gender identity, and gender expression. In a study commissioned by GLSEN, 80 percent of parents favor expanding existing antiharassment and antidiscrimination policies to include GLBTQ students. The study also showed that 80 percent of parents support teacher sensitivity trainings on tolerance that include instructions on dealing with gay and lesbian harassment in schools, 63 percent favor including positive information about gays and lesbians in middle and high school health and sex education classes, and 60 percent favor including information about transgender people in those forums.

It's a tough battle, but these efforts have resulted in real accomplishments. Some school boards have added sexual orientation and gender identity to their codes of conduct. That means students, faculty, and staff are barred from discriminating against others who are or who are perceived to be GLBTQ. These rules usually already include descriptors such as race, gender, religious affiliation, disability, and more.

▼ **Bullying vs. Harassment** What is the difference between bullying and harassment? It can be hard to tell because both involve behavior that is intended to undermine, victimize, humiliate, threaten, or harm someone. The primary difference is that whereas harassment could be a single incident (or a few isolated incidents), bullying generally involves repeatedly and directly targeting an individual with malicious behavior over time. ▼

Some schools sponsor assemblies to educate students about GLBTQ people, while others now allow gay pride month displays. Some students form gay-straight alliance clubs (GSAs) to educate others in their schools and work for change.

In 2010, GLBTQ Online High School (www.glbtqonlinehigh school.com) opened its virtual doors. In addition to providing a full online education for students, the school is reaching out to traditional public schools and helping provide information on and tools for creating a more supportive and safer learning environment for GLBTQ students.

A large "safe schools" movement is underway to end bullying and help GLBTQ students feel welcome and secure at school, but if you're being bullied or otherwise discriminated against now, it might feel like it will be forever until things change at your school. What can you do to advocate for yourself?

Responding to Homophobia

Understanding homophobia and where it comes from is one thing; figuring out what you're going to do about bullying or harassment is another.

Prejudice can show itself in many ways. A GLBTQ teen might be cut from a sports team or dubbed a "troublemaker" by teachers. An administrator could turn a blind eye to bullying or tell a student that he brought it on himself. There are a number of possible ways to react to such incidents, ranging from ignoring them to confronting the people involved.

How Bullying and Harassment Can Make You Feel

Dealing with ongoing harassment and ignorance can make you feel scared, isolated, depressed, angry, or just plain worn out. Sometimes it may feel like fighting homophobia is an uphill battle, like things will never get better. Even if you feel comfortable with being GLBTQ and good about yourself overall, facing regular harassment can be demoralizing.

As you'll see in the sections that follow, you can address homophobia in many ways. Regardless of how you decide to handle it, it's important to remember that you're not to blame for the bad treatment you're receiving, and you're not alone in experiencing homophobia. *Homophobia is not about you—it's about other people.*

Even if you understand that homophobia isn't your fault, it can still hurt. It's important to engage in activities that make you feel good about yourself. Writing, drawing, dancing, working out, or hanging out with friends are all great options. Take time to check in with yourself every so often to make sure that homophobia isn't hurting your self-esteem. For more information on being healthy and feeling good about who you are, see Chapter 8 (page 129).

In addressing homophobia, it's important to understand that you can't control the words and actions of other people. So focus on what you can control, which is your response to those words and actions. In determining how best to respond, consider several issues.

Assessing the Situation

Safety must be your number one concern. Before you decide how to react to homophobia, assess the situation.

1. Is the person merely being ignorant? Or do they mean to do you some kind of harm? Sometimes it's hard to tell, sometimes it's fairly apparent.

2. Is the person aggressive with her words or body language? Is she threatening you, using a threatening tone, or moving closer to you? Don't discount your gut instinct—it's usually your best indicator. If you feel even the least bit afraid, proceed with caution.
3. Has this person harassed you before? If so, has there been an escalation in the harassment? (Perhaps a taunt in the hallway has turned into shoving or worse.)
4. Are you alone or do you have friends with you? Is there an adult nearby who could help?
5. Where are you? Can you get away? It's important to always know where your exits are.

Homophobia stirs up a lot of emotions. Even so, it's important to look at the situation rather than react based on your feelings. Maybe the girl in your class wasn't trying to be mean when she made that comment, she just didn't realize how it sounded. But the bully who throws stuff at you might become increasingly violent in the future.

BEEN THERE

"My parents signed me up for karate a couple years ago because I was getting harassed at school. It was scary at first because I didn't know much about it, but now I love it. It's made me more fit and more confident. It's also helped me be a better judge of when a situation might be dangerous so I can either avoid it entirely or get to safety." —Carlos, 16

Options for Responding

The first option is to turn the other cheek. That's hard to do, because encountering homophobia can be so frustrating. Sometimes what you really feel like doing is lashing out, but try to consider the safest, most productive, and most effective ways to respond.

Some people use humor to help them turn the other cheek or to diffuse the situation. You can also ignore homophobia completely by acting like you didn't hear the remark or by not reacting to the sign stuck on your backpack; instead, just throw it away. But ignoring and forgiving homophobia can be extremely difficult, and it's rarely an option if you're placed in a dangerous situation.

BEEN THERE

"I was just doing my thing at my locker when one of a group of girls looked at me and said, 'You're a dyke.' I looked back at her and smiled and said, 'You say that like it's a bad thing.' She was stunned. She just looked at me for a minute, then turned and walked away." —Anna, 17

Speaking Up

Speaking up is another option. Again, consider the situation—responding to homophobia should be limited to situations when it would be, or at least could be, productive. (Sometimes productive simply means it makes *you* feel better.) If you keep your wits about you, you can sometimes turn a negative situation into a more positive one by speaking up when someone demonstrates homophobia.

If you decide to respond to someone who's being homophobic, here are a few ground rules that can help achieve a positive result:

1. Don't match insult for insult. This will only escalate the situation.

▼ **Coming Together to Fight Homophobia** In 2009, several schools in Maryland were the targets of protests by a religious group from Topeka, Kansas. Students and community members mobilized to counter the protests. At Walt Whitman High School, the group of seven congregants from Kansas protested because the school was named after a gay poet. At the 2:10 dismissal, 500 students lined up and faced the group of seven from Kansas and chanted the name of their high school and "Go home!" Some students wore T-shirts with Walt Whitman's famous words, "Let your soul stand cool and composed."

The protestors later went to Montgomery Blair High School to demonstrate against the school's gay-straight alliance (GSA). A local open congregation launched a fundraiser in response, encouraging churchgoers to donate money for every minute the Kansas group protested the school. The church donated the money to a local gay rights organization. ▼

2. Try to get the person to name her behavior by asking in a nonconfrontational tone (if you can manage it), "Why would you say something like that?" or "Are you aware that sounds homophobic?" or something similar.
3. State how the comments or actions make you feel instead of something negative about the person who said them. Instead of saying, "You're only saying that because you're ignorant," try, "There are a lot of misconceptions about queer people. We're all human beings, and it can really hurt to hear those kinds of things."
4. If a person becomes (or is already) threatening or aggressive, get yourself out of the situation as quickly and calmly as possible.

There may be times when it's appropriate just to turn around and say, "I really didn't appreciate that comment." However, if you're going to respond to homophobia, include something constructive. Tell the person why you don't appreciate his comments or how the comments or actions make you feel, but keep your cool while you're doing it. Homophobia is an issue that's easy to get upset about. A comment you intended to be constructive could escalate into a fight. In the heat of the moment, it can be tough to think of something to say beyond four-letters words.

BEEN THERE

"When I was in tenth grade, a teacher mentioned something about there being gay students at our school and the girl I was sitting next to asked, 'There are gay people in this school?' The guy sitting next to her, the girl sitting in front of her, and I all turned and said 'yes' at the same time. By my twelfth-grade year, no one would ask that question." —Alex, 19

Following are some common homophobic remarks, along with possible responses. Some are humorous, some are not, but all are designed to make people think about what they said. In each case, you can customize responses based on whether someone is addressing your sexual orientation or gender identity.

When someone tells a homophobic joke.
Possible response: "When you tell jokes like that, you give the impression that it's okay to make fun of GLBTQ people. Is that what you really believe?"

"He's such a fag," or "You look like a dyke."
Possible response: "How would you feel if I called you a 'breeder' or a 'hetero'?" or "What's with the hate?"

"Ugh, that's so gay. Oh, you know, I don't mean it that way. It's just an expression."
Possible response: "It's still hurtful to hear," or "I understand what you're saying, but if you don't mean it that way, maybe another expression that doesn't insult people would be more appropriate," or even, "Maybe you don't mean it that way, but that's how a lot of people hear it. Are you okay with people thinking you're homophobic?"

"What do queer people do in bed?"
Possible response: "Sleep. Sometimes we watch TV or read."

"You don't *look* gay."
Possible response: "That's because I'm one of our secret agents. It's such a relief to know the disguise is working," or "What does gay look like to you?"

To a girl: "You just haven't met the right guy yet."
Possible response to another girl: "Maybe you just haven't met the right girl yet."

"You're just going through a phase."
Possible response: "Is my entire life a phase?" or "I know I'm gay in the same way you know you're straight."

"Queer people spread AIDS."
Possible response: "According to the National Institutes of Health, the highest transmission rates are among heterosexuals."

"Why do gay people have to flaunt who they are?"
Possible response: "Refusing to hide is not flaunting," or "I'm just being me."

"People like you are disgusting."
Possible response: "Ignorance and hatred are disgusting."
Another option when you hear a homophobic remark or question
is to name it. Say, "That comment is homophobic," or even ask,
"What is it about queer people that makes you so afraid?"

Try to Educate Others

Although it can be satisfying to give a cutting reply, it's not
necessarily going to inspire a change in behavior. Another option,
which goes hand-in-hand with speaking up, is trying to turn the
incident into an educational opportunity. You can address the
roots of homophobia by asking something like, "What ideas do
you have about gay people that make you say that?"

Realistically, this approach will be more effective with friends
and acquaintances than with someone who is threatening to
hurt you. Also, people are more likely to engage in a conversation
when they're not surrounded by a group of their friends, who
might be egging them on. Use your judgment. Not everyone will
be receptive, but even if someone doesn't react positively right
away, down the road she might think about what you said and it
might have a more lasting and positive effect.

Some people don't even realize that things they say are offensive. It can be particularly painful when a friend or family member makes negative comments or jokes about GLBTQ people.
Some people ask personal questions that they wouldn't ask their
straight friends, and that can be offensive, too. So sometimes it's
good to engage people about their comment instead of zinging
them and walking away. They could learn something.

Fighting Homophobia Through Activism

Like George Loomis, Jacob Sullivan, and other teens who have
taken formal action to end harassment and educate others,
young people all over are working to create change locally and
nationally. Steven Cozza, an Eagle Scout and professional cyclist,
took on the entire Boy Scouts of America when he was just 12
years old. Steven's willingness to speak out against homophobia
in Scouting ignited a national movement. His group, Scouting for
All, continues to advocate for gay Scouts.

You can make a difference in a lot of ways. Maybe you'll decide to join or start a GSA or another GLBTQ group at school. Or you might get involved with a local or national organization. Groups like GLSEN, GLAAD, and HRC, to name just a few, are always happy for more volunteers. They also can provide you with ideas about things you can do to make your own area or school a friendlier place for queer people.

BEEN THERE

"One year we organized a National Coming Out Day event, which consisted of putting up posters and handing out rainbow stickers. It was great. There were rainbows all over the school, including on many people's backpacks who I'd never even met! But best of all, people stopped using 'gay' as an all-purpose insult. When people started to realize that they knew gay people and that gay people were being affected by slurs, a lot of people stopped using them." — Jan, 19

"I got involved with a group called Lambda . . . which had a speakers' bureau. We would go to high schools and middle schools and talk to students and teachers about our experiences coming out and answer questions that they had." — Nancy, 19

Getting involved and working for change not only can produce a positive result, but it may also help you feel better about yourself and the homophobia you might be facing. Dealing with ignorance again and again can be depressing, frustrating, and isolating; at times, you might even feel helpless against it. Getting involved in GLBTQ causes can empower you to change your world. It's also a great way to gain support and meet other GLBTQ people and individuals who are open-minded.

Being an activist can be a very consuming experience. Be sure to make time for yourself, your schoolwork, your job, your friends, and any other positive things you have in your life.

When Homophobia = Ongoing Harassment

Sometimes homophobia reveals itself in harassment, which can take the form of bullying, either in person, online (cyberbullying), or a combination of the two. Not just a remark here or there (although those remarks can hurt), but constant badgering, escalating teasing, or physical threats. Bullying and harassment are not okay, and you don't have to live with it.

GLSEN advises students to document incidents of bullying. Write down who did or said what, when, and where. Note anyone who was there and witnessed the incident. And keep it all together in a file or notebook. That way when you report it, you have a written record of exactly what happened. Also keep a written record of who you report the harassment to, what you said, where you talked, and when the meeting happened. This information especially comes in handy if there is no follow-through from the person or people you tell.

So who do you tell about bullying? Reporting it to an approachable teacher, counselor, or administrator are all options. Maybe one of your teachers or a school staff member has witnessed the bullying and will support you if you go to the administration.

It can be very daunting to approach an administrator. Not only are you upset about the incident or incidents, you might also be worried about the administrator's reaction. It's even tougher if you aren't comfortable being GLBTQ or talking about it. For that reason, it's a good idea to get a parent or another adult to go with you. This person can support you, and her presence can help show the administrator that bullying is a serious matter and won't be tolerated.

BEEN THERE

"The majority of my attackers were never punished. On one occasion, three boys were suspended for three days. The principal told me they were suspended for the verbal attacks and not the physical one, as the physical one could not be proven. I had several witnesses report it to him, but he just didn't want to do much about it. Later, I was attacked in the hallway. I do not remember much of it, as my head was hit on the locker several times and I must have blacked out or something. After that, I got a lawyer through the ACLU and a couple of national organizations helped me by talking with school officials. The school has been very supportive recently. Maybe that was because of my influence and pressure on them." —Randy, 15

Here are some tips for approaching a school official or other adult:

1. Stay calm. If you present your case in a calm, rational way, it will be harder for the adult to dismiss you as overreacting or being too emotional.
2. Provide an exact account, as detailed as you can remember, about what happened. It's also helpful if you have witnesses who are willing to back up your story.
3. Explain that your safety is in jeopardy as long as the issue continues unaddressed.

Some school officials will be outraged by the harassment. Others will be reluctant to take action. Some might imply or say outright that GLBTQ students invite harassment by being out. If you are assaulted (the legal definition is a threat of harm) or battered (physically attacked), you can file a report with the police. If no one will help you, you can reach out to a national organization like GLSEN or the National Gay and Lesbian Task

Force (NGLTF). There also might be a local group in your area that can help you. Either way, you don't have to accept harassment, and you don't have to confront it alone.

The Cyberbullying Epidemic

It has come to light that many of the GLBTQ teens who committed suicide recently were the victims of cyberbullying. The popularity of social media sites and use of text messaging has resulted in an increase of cyberbullying. According to GLSEN's "2009 National School Climate Survey," 53 percent of students reported having been victims of cyberbullying.

Cyberbullying can take place via electronic means and forums such as email, chat rooms, social media pages, instant messaging, text messaging, and blogs.

According to the Stop Bullying Now project (www.stop bullyingnow.hrsa.gov/kids), cyberbullying includes:
- Sending mean, vulgar, or threatening messages or images
- Posting sensitive, private information and/or lies about another person
- Pretending to be someone else in order to make another person look bad
- Intentionally excluding someone from an online group

This form of harassment can be particularly tough to deal with because messages communicated electronically often can be quickly and broadly distributed, and it's not always easy to tell who is sending the messages.

Putting an end to cyberbullying involves many of the same steps as stopping in-person harassment. The National Crime Prevention Council (NCPC) advises young people to tell a trusted adult about the harassment so she or he can help get the proper authorities involved. In the case of online harassment, the NCPC also encourages you to report the abuse to site administrators and to use online tools to block hurtful messages. In severe cases, changing your email address or phone number is suggested.

If it becomes necessary to involve law enforcement or other officials, you will want a record of the bullying. As much as you might want to delete the offensive messages, it's a good idea to keep them to document and prove what's happened. Also, if you are not sure who is harassing you, electronic messages often can be traced back to the source.

The Good News

Although a lot of negativity exists toward GLBTQ people, the world continues to change for the better. Not all (or even most) straight people are anti-gay. Young people are helping to make the biggest difference when it comes to promoting positive attitudes about GLBTQ people. A Gallup poll conducted in May of each year asks Americans about their attitudes toward homosexuality. In 2008, 57 percent of all Americans surveyed said they found homosexuality to be an acceptable lifestyle, compared with only 34 percent in 1982. Acceptance of GLBTQ people is even higher among younger generations—75 percent of Americans ages 18 to 34 surveyed said they feel homosexuality is acceptable.

While it's likely you'll encounter homophobia in your life, you will also—and hopefully far more often—encounter acceptance.

▼ Help for Harassment

Gay, Lesbian and Straight Education Network (GLSEN)
(212) 727-0135 • www.glsen.org
GLSEN works to create safe schools for all GLBTQ people, but especially students. The organization's website offers a variety of resources and information on safe schools efforts, including gay-straight alliances (GSAs) and anti-discrimination legislation. It also includes information specific to stopping anti-GLBTQ bullying.

Human Rights Campaign (HRC)
1-800-777-4723 • www.hrc.org
The Human Rights Campaign works to protect the rights of GLBTQ people and improve their quality of life. The group is a resource for the latest information on GLBTQ legislative issues and campaigns such as National Coming Out Day.

National Gay and Lesbian Task Force (NGLTF)
(202) 393-5177 • www.thetaskforce.org
The NGLTF works at the local, state, and national levels to fight prejudice and violence against queer people. The organization provides many services including legal assistance and referrals to other professionals.

Parents, Families and Friends of Lesbians and Gays (PFLAG)
(202) 467-8180 • www.pflag.org
PFLAG provides materials and support services for queer people and their families.

It Gets Better Project
www.itgetsbetterproject.com
Does it ever seem like bullying and harassment will never end? It's natural to have this fear, but life does get better. If you'd like some proof, check out this website to watch videos from GLBTQ people and supporters offering perspective and encouragement.

Stop Bullying Now
www.stopbullyingnow.hrsa.gov/kids
A project of the U.S. Health Resources and Services Administration, Stop Bullying Now is a resource designed to help young people end bullying. The site includes an ask-the-expert section, tips, video features, and specific information on cyberbullying.

American Civil Liberties Union (ACLU)
(212) 549-2500 • www.aclu.org
The ACLU works in the courts to defend civil liberties for all people, including those who are GLBTQ. It has an extensive track record of advocating for GLBTQ rights. ▼

Chapter 3

Coming Out

We're here. We're queer. Get used to it.

Throughout history, GLBTQ people have often felt the need to hide who they are to avoid harassment and discrimination. However, a gradual shift in society's attitudes toward GLBTQ people has been occurring. This shift, combined with turning-point events like the 1969 Stonewall riots, has helped create an atmosphere where more people feel comfortable coming out. Many GLBTQ people used to hide their identities, but today, more and more are open about who they are.

On one level, coming out is very simple. It's nothing more than being open with family, friends,

Stonewall
In June of 1969, a group of GLBTQ people stood up to police harassment at the Stonewall Inn in New York City. This event is widely viewed as the start of an organized gay rights movement in the United States. Commemorations of the Stonewall riots eventually turned into the GLBTQ pride celebrations that take place across the country every June. The event has been memorialized in books and even a movie.

and others about identifying as GLBTQ. On another level, coming out isn't so simple. It can expose you to everything from awkward social situations, such as someone trying to fix you up with the only other queer person he knows, to prejudice and harassment.

BEEN THERE

"As a freshman in college I came out to a friend of mine. At first, I thought it might be a big mistake because she was the most popular freshman on campus. But I thought that since she trusted me with her deepest secrets, then I could trust her with mine. When I told her she said, 'Wow, that's cool. You know, I didn't want to ask but. . . .' That was the beginning of our friendship on a whole new level." —Sasha, 20

The decision to come out is a significant one, especially when you're a teen. Some teens who come out are harassed and experience violence at home or at school. Some teens are kicked out of the house or are forced to run away. These things don't happen to everyone, but it's important to seriously consider your safety and well-being before coming out.

But coming out also has many positive aspects. You can live your life openly and meet other GLBTQ people. Many GLBTQ teens say being out feels liberating. It can be very empowering to be honest about who you are. *American Idol* finalist Adam Lambert spoke publicly about the relief he felt after coming out in an interview with *Rolling Stone* magazine. He initially tried to hide that he was gay because he feared it would hurt his chances of winning *American Idol*.

The purpose of this chapter is not to tell you whether or not you should come out—it's to help you decide what's right for you. Even if you don't feel like you have a lot of control over your life, *you* are the only person who can ultimately decide how to live it. That includes making decisions about how out you want to be. If you do decide to come out, this chapter will give you some advice on how best to do it.

What Is Coming Out All About?

As you learn more about the GLBTQ community, you'll find that coming out is a very meaningful issue. Some people will ask you if you're out, or who you're out to. They might want to share their coming-out stories. Sometimes it seems like everyone who is GLBTQ is obsessed with the idea of being out. A popular GLBTQ magazine is called *Out,* and there's even a National Coming Out Project.

Coming out is the process of telling others that you're GLBTQ. The phrase "coming out" comes from the metaphor that you're "coming out of the closet." Conversely, people who are not out often are referred to as being "closeted," meaning they've chosen not to tell others of their GLBTQ identity.

There's a whole range of being out. People can be completely out, meaning they're open with everyone about being GLBTQ. Some are partially out, meaning they're out to some people but not everyone. Others might only be out to one very close person in their lives. Some people aren't out at all.

Coming out has its pluses and minuses. It can open up your social life to other GLBTQ teens and allow you to live openly without having to hide who you are. But it can also cause stress in your family and put a strain on some of your friendships. For most GLBTQ people, coming out is a major milestone and a life-changing experience. It's like taking off a mask and letting people see who you really are. Some people decide to come out because they're tired of hiding who they are. These people are willing to risk telling others in exchange for the freedom of living openly.

▼ **Queer in the Military** During World War II, if military personnel were discovered to be GLBTQ, they were given special dishonorable discharges called "blue discharges" (because the form on which they were typed was blue). People who received blue discharges often had trouble finding employment and faced rejection in civilian life. Although GLBTQ people in the military were, until recently, forced to hide their sexual orientations and gender identities, many queer people have served their country in the armed forces, some receiving the military's highest honors. For more information on the military's "Don't Ask, Don't Tell" policy, see page 21 in Chapter 1. ▼

Feeling Pressure to Come Out

All of this emphasis on coming out can put a lot of pressure on you, but there's no rush. People can be ready to come out at different times. Some come out at 14, others at 40. Coming out can be a great and affirming experience. But if you're not ready, it can feel like a disaster.

Dr. Sandy Loiterstein, a clinical psychologist who often works with GLBTQ people, emphasizes this point. She explains, "It's important for teens to know that discovering your identity is a process, and everyone does so in her own time. Teens, especially, can have a tough time figuring out who they are because they are sorting through so many issues at once."

You might feel internal pressure to come out, or see out celebrities or people in your community and think, "I *should* be out." You can also feel pressure from other sources, such as friends or people in the GLBTQ community. Some people might be saying you need to come out, but others might be giving you completely different messages. Maybe your parents or other people say things like, "I don't understand why gay people have to flaunt it. They should just keep it to themselves." Regardless of what others tell you, your first responsibility is to yourself.

How's the Weather Out There? Deciding If You're Ready (and If It's Safe) to Come Out

Without a doubt, more teens than ever are coming out. Many studies, news articles, and books are noting the increasingly younger ages when people are coming out. According to Cornell University professor Ritch Savin-Williams, a recognized authority on issues surrounding GLBTQ teens, the current generation of teens self-identifies as gay, lesbian, bisexual, or something else other than straight on average at around 16 years old. This is down from an average age of 21 two to three decades ago. In his book *The New Gay Teenager,* Savin-Williams also notes that today's teenage girls are less likely to identify as lesbian, instead identifying frequently as bisexual, polysexual, omnisexual, or some other term suggesting they are not exclusively attracted to females or males.

A 2009 cover story in *The New York Times Magazine* focused on young people coming out in middle school, including a boy who decided to come out at age 11. The article suggests that earlier sexual development and increased exposure to positive information about being GLBTQ could be factors in this phenomenon.

But some people question whether a person has the ability to be certain of her orientation at such a young age. "How can you possibly know at that age?" is a common question.

Many GLBTQ young people today don't identify as one thing or another. Instead, they're comfortable existing in an open space or gray area when it comes to sexual orientation. "Who cares about labels?" is a common attitude among these teens. GLBTQ teens typically have more straight allies among peers than in previous generations, and that can help them feel more comfortable coming out or identifying as something other than gay or lesbian.

This fluidity in the way some people define their orientation can confuse those who are used to black and white notions of "gay" and "straight." The idea of sexual attraction and orientation without boundaries or distinctions isn't really different from the sexual orientation spectrum documented by Alfred Kinsey (see page 10).

Many young people do choose to come out, but that doesn't mean you have to. In fact, in some cases, coming out might not be the best decision, at least for now. Tom Sauerman, a leader in the Philadelphia chapter of PFLAG, advises that it might be better for some teens to wait to come out until they can be reasonably certain it won't jeopardize their safety or quality of life at home or school.

Questions to Ask Yourself Before Coming Out

Only you can decide the right time to come out. So it's up to you to make sure you're ready. If you are emotionally prepared to come out, you'll have a more positive experience than if you're not. Here are some questions to ask yourself about being ready.

Am I sure I'm GLBTQ? If you're not certain you are GLBTQ (and remember, it's okay to be questioning), you might want to wait before coming out. Most GLBTQ people come out in part because they feel the need to have others know what they're feeling and experiencing. If you're not sure whether you're GLBTQ, think about waiting. Or you can come out as queer or "not straight" rather than choosing a label. But you might have more explaining to do in this situation, because most people have a better understanding of terms like gay, lesbian, bisexual, or transgender than broader ideas such as queer, genderqueer, or "other."

Am I comfortable with myself? This can be a challenge. After all, you might feel what every teenager feels at one time or another—that there's nothing comfortable about being you. This could be because of your sexual orientation, or it could just be part of adjusting to changes in your body and your social roles. If you're comfortable with yourself and confident about your orientation (whether it's a distinct label or not), the person you're coming out to is more likely to be accepting of you.

Why am I coming out? Come out because you're ready. Come out to affirm yourself. Come out because you want to share with others who you are. In short, come out because *you want to*. Don't come out on a whim, to get a reaction from someone, or because anyone else is pressuring you.

Can I be patient with other people's reactions? It's natural to want an immediate positive reaction from the person you're coming out to, but that probably won't always be the case. Remember how long it might have taken you to adjust to the idea that you're GLBTQ. Others may need time to adjust, too. Be mentally prepared to give them that time.

The World Around You: An Essential Checklist

Even if you're emotionally ready, there are also some external factors that could influence whether it's a good idea to come out:

1. Is it safe for you to come out? If GLBTQ people are openly harassed or threatened where you live or go to school and there isn't protection from abuse, it might not be safe for you to come out. According to GLSEN's "2009 National School Climate Survey," 61 percent of respondents reported feeling unsafe at school because of their sexual orientation.

BEEN THERE

"Don't get me wrong. I'm proud of who I am. I just have to be proud quietly because I live in a very small (and small-minded) community. Just last year at my school, a boy who people called gay was beaten within an inch of his life. I'm a little scared to be too public about it for now." —Calista, 19

2. What is your home environment like? If your parents or guardians are aggressive or otherwise abusive, coming out to them could escalate the abuse. If adults at home are extremely homophobic, you might also decide to wait to come out until you have left home or at least have other options if needed. But some teens, who feel safe and comfortable doing so, come out to family adults. People at home can be a source of support and help teens deal with harassment from others.

In the previously mentioned *New York Times Magazine* cover story about gay teens, the author quotes openly gay boys' varsity soccer coach Dan Woog: "The biggest difference I've seen in the last 10 years isn't with gay kids—it's with their families. . . . Many parents just don't assume anymore that their kids will have a sad, difficult life just because they're gay."

> **A Nationwide Campaign**
> Coming Out Project (www.hrc.org/issues/coming_out). Sponsored by the Human Rights Campaign, this initiative provides resources on coming out. For information on deciding whether it's the right time to come out, guidance on how to do it, and much more, visit the website or call 1-800-777-4723.

3. Do you have a support system? Do you have someone to turn to if the reaction to your coming out is bad? You might have a friend who already knows who can support you. Also, there are groups that can help.

If You Don't Have a Choice: Being Outed

Some teens don't get a choice about coming out. A parent might notice on the computer that you've visited GLBTQ websites. A classmate might overhear a conversation you had with a friend. It's possible to be outed without your consent.

Being outed can be challenging because you have to deal with being out right away—without warning or time to plan. You might suddenly find yourself in an unsafe position. Or family members or friends could say they support you no matter what. Chances are the reality will be somewhere in between.

BEEN THERE

"I was only 13 when I got into a fight with my mom about a letter of mine she'd found. She had the nerve to tell me to stop acting so 'cuddly' with my girlfriends. 'It's not like you're a lesbian are you?' she shouted. Then and there I told her I was bisexual. She stormed from the room. The following day she admitted that it troubled her and that it would take a little while to get used to it, but she wasn't angry or disappointed in me." —Erin, 19

Now What? Some Tips for Outed Teens

Being outed can feel like a nightmare. Or it can come as a great relief. People don't always react as negatively as you think they might (although sometimes the opposite is true). They might even be positive and supportive.

Still, any situation you're not in control of can be scary. So what do you do if you're outed?

1. Take a deep breath. Being outed can be very unsettling because you weren't given a choice about it. You might feel like you weren't ready to come out. But it happened, so take a moment to regroup and think about how you want to deal with the situation. It's true that you weren't able to control being outed, but you can control how you deal with it from here.

2. Assess the situation. Take a look around to determine what your next move should be. Are you safe? How do you feel? How are others reacting? These questions can help you figure out whether you should try to start a conversation right now or regroup before going forward. You might want to get outside resources and/or help.

3. Take action. Based on the other person's reaction and your level of preparedness, you have several options. If you feel like you can engage in a conversation, try it. By opening the lines of communication, you're taking back some degree of control over the situation, and that can be very empowering. It can also help increase the odds of a positive outcome from the situation.

If the situation is too emotionally charged to engage in a positive conversation, or if a discussion starts to get too heated, you can initiate a cooling-off period. This could be a good opportunity for you to chat with a friend, talk to an adult you trust, or reach out to a GLBTQ group for guidance and support.

A third course of action might be more of a necessity than an option. If being outed has made you fear for your safety, either at home or elsewhere, you may need to get immediate help. It's a good idea to approach an adult for assistance—a trusted family member, neighbor, counselor, or school official. You could also contact a GLBTQ group that supports teens. Many such organizations are listed in the Resources (page 207).

Why Come Out?

People come out for a variety of reasons, and many of them are quite positive. Coming out is a way to affirm yourself. It shows others that you're happy with who you are. It can also be a way to reach out to others by sharing something very meaningful and personal with them.

Some people come out to increase the overall visibility of GLBTQ people and help advance the GLBTQ human rights movement. Right now, society as a whole assumes that most people are straight (an attitude called "heterosexism"). Many straight people look at others around them and, in the absence of any obvious indication otherwise, assume everyone they see is also straight. Coming out and doing things like wearing a queer-themed shirt or putting a rainbow sticker on your car are ways of challenging these assumptions.

BEEN THERE
"There were 1,900 students at my school when I graduated—1,900 people who can't assume or pretend that gay people don't exist. And if you look at statistics that as many as 10 percent of people are queer, that means that when I came out there were maybe 190 queer kids who got to hear that they are not going to burn in hell, that they are not perverts, and that they can live their lives."
—Anthony, 19

Who Should I Tell First?

Many people start the coming out process by telling only one or two people, sort of like dipping your big toe into a pool to test the water. Others choose to tell a lot of people all at once. Many decide to come out to a friend or sibling first because they believe they'll get a better reaction from him or her than they might from a parent.

It's definitely a good idea to choose someone you think will be supportive. For some, parents or other family adults are the last people they want to tell. For others, adults at home are people they feel they can go to with anything and who they want to come out to first.

BEEN THERE
"I have come out to my brother. He is younger than me by a year. I felt like I needed to tell someone close to me, and he was the one. . . . It has brought us closer." —Athena, 20

There are two big reasons why it's important to take care in selecting the first person (or people) you come out to. For starters, if you have a positive first experience, you'll feel better about the prospect of coming out to other people. Having someone react positively is a boost to your self-esteem.

Second, if the first person you come out to is accepting of you, then you have additional support as you come out to others. You'll have someone you can talk to about how you're feeling. This person can also be someone you practice on when you're preparing to come out to others. It's very comforting to have someone you can be honest with.

▼ **Straight Allies** "My husband and I put a Human Rights Campaign sticker on our car because we have a lot of gay friends, and we want them and other gay people to know that we support them. It's important for us that gay people know that not all straight people are against them." —Shari, 42 ▼

I Have Something to Tell You: Coming Out to Your Family

You've given it a lot of thought and you feel you're ready to come out. So how do you do it, especially to (gulp) your family? There are a lot of possibilities for doing this. While there isn't one perfect method for coming out, some ways are more likely to have a positive outcome.

Be Prepared

Do your research. Start by testing your family members' reactions to GLBTQ people. Mention a GLBTQ character on a popular TV show. Bring up an issue like GLBTQ civil rights or queer people being allowed to adopt children and see what their reactions are. Keep in mind—these are only hints. Even if parents, siblings, or grandparents say GLBTQ people should have equal rights, that doesn't mean they'll be totally calm when they find out it's their own relative they're talking about. And the opposite could be true. Knowing a family member is queer might encourage them to think about what it means to be GLBTQ in a different, more positive way.

Gather resources from groups like HRC, PFLAG, and GLSEN (see pages 210–211). These and other GLBTQ organizations have reading lists and brochures for both you and your family. Even if family members don't read the brochures or visit the websites you give them right away, they might later. And while you might feel awkward about coming out to people and then handing them reading material, they're more likely to read something you give them than they are to do research on their own. It's an opportunity for you to give them information that is positive and accurate.

Be patient. Coming out to family members—especially those closest to you—is a milestone in your life. It's a big deal for them, too. It can be tough, even heartbreaking, when someone you really care about has trouble accepting who you are. But give family members the benefit of the doubt if they don't embrace your sexual orientation or gender identity at first. Remember that you've had a lot longer to adjust to and accept yourself as GLBTQ. Chances are it's breaking news to them.

▼ **Coming Out as Questioning . . . or as Something Else Entirely** You might decide to come out to someone as questioning. Or maybe you want to come out as omnisexual, genderqueer, or some other term you're comfortable with. If you do, you'll probably have to answer a lot of questions—perhaps even more. Saying that you identify as questioning might be confusing for people who need labels like straight, gay, lesbian, bisexual, or transgender to help them understand the situation. That means a lot of people probably won't understand what you mean when you say you're questioning (or however you choose to describe yourself).

Many people prefer to come out after they have a more concrete concept of their sexual orientation or gender identity. For others, coming out as questioning helps them gain support from friends or family members as they go through the process of exploring their identities. Still others will keep some fluidity and choose to never label themselves as one specific orientation.

However you decide to come out (*if* you decide to come out), remember to keep the lines of communication open and try to be patient with others' questions. More often than not, they're just trying to understand you better—and that's a sign that they care. ▼

Pick a good time. Coming out to a parent, grandparent, or another family adult the minute he comes home from work or at the big family holiday dinner is probably a bad idea. Avoid situations that already are stressful. Again, keep in mind that you've been adjusting to the idea of being queer for a while, but it might come as a complete surprise to others. Pick a time when everyone seems relaxed and comfortable.

Hope for the best, but prepare for the worst. Some family members might respond by kicking you out of your home. It sounds harsh, but it does happen. Have an idea of where you can go or who you can turn to if things get ugly at home.

Practice. Once you've decided you want to come out, practice, practice, practice. Look at yourself in the mirror or practice on the poster of your favorite musician or sports figure. It's like giving a presentation at school, only much more personal. You might think it's weird to practice. But it's an emotional topic and it might be more difficult than you think to express yourself. If you practice what you're going to say, you'll probably sound a lot calmer and clearer when the time arrives. As you practice, try to anticipate some of the questions people might ask so you have well-thought-out responses. See the following section for some common reactions and responses you can provide.

Having "The Talk"

No matter how much you prepare, there's no telling what your family members' reactions will be. Nevertheless, parents and others have very common reactions and questions in response to a loved one coming out. It may help to keep the following reactions in mind as you prepare for "The Talk." State your responses as calmly and rationally as possible so you don't ignite an altercation. It can be really difficult not to get worked up when you feel strongly about something, but that won't help your case.

Coming Out Checklist

If you haven't checked off each of these, you might want to rethink your decision to come out.

- ☑ I am ready and I am comfortable with myself.

- ☑ I've asked myself why I want to come out, and I'm sure it's for the right reasons.

- ☑ I'm ready to deal with the outcome and realize it might not be the outcome I predict.

- ☑ I'm ready to provide information and answer questions.

- ☑ I have a support system in case this doesn't go the way I'd like it to.

Reaction: "How do you know?"
Possible response: "How do you know you're straight? It's just something I feel deep inside."

Reaction: "It's just a phase" or "You're too young to know."
Possible response: "I understand that you're probably surprised by this. This isn't a phase, and I think in time you'll realize that. I know I might seem too young to know for sure, but think about how old you were when you started to get crushes on other boys or girls and develop more meaningful attractions. Me being

queer is new to you, but my understanding of who I am has been evolving in me for a long time."

Reaction: "Why are you doing this to me?"
Possible response: "This isn't about you. It's about me and my relationship with you. I'm telling you this because it's who I am and I respect and want to be open with you. I want you to have a relationship with *me*, not the person you *think* I am, and that means I have to be honest with you."

Reaction: "It's your choice to be this way."
Possible response: "No one knows exactly why people are queer, but most scientists and health professionals believe that part of it could be biology. I don't have those kinds of answers for you, but what I can tell you is that for me, I don't feel it's a choice. This is just who I am."

Reaction: "You're just saying that because you think it's cool."
Possible response: "Cool is about what other people think of you. It's just an opinion. This isn't about what anyone else thinks is cool or not cool, it's about who I am."

Reaction: "But your life is going to be so hard."
Possible response: "Life can be more difficult for GLBTQ people at times, sure. I'll have to deal with other people's prejudice and ignorance, but I can handle that. What's more difficult to deal with is prejudice in my own family, and that's why I need your support. Besides, life is challenging for everyone at one time or another. That's why we need to stick together."

Reaction: "Why do you want to live that way?"
Possible response: "There's no 'way' GLBTQ people live. We're just like everyone else. The queer community is just as diverse in our lifestyles and opinions as the straight community. A lot of stereotypes exist about the so-called 'queer lifestyle,' but they're just stereotypes."

Reaction: "I always thought you'd get married and have children."
Possible response: "Maybe someday I *will* get married, if I find the right person and that's what my partner and I want. And if we want children, we can do that, too. Lots of parents today are the same sex."

Reaction: "It's just wrong."

Possible response: "Who I am is not wrong. I think that lying to you is wrong, and that's why I want to be open with you about this. I care about you and what you think is important to me, so it's painful for me to hear that you feel that way. But I also understand that this is a lot of information to take in, and you probably need some time to think about it. But please know that you can bring it up later and we can talk about it. Just know that I'm telling you this out of love and respect for you and our relationship."

BEEN THERE

"My father's response was simple. He stood up, gave me a hug, and said, 'You remember I said I would always love you, right?' I said, 'Yes.' And he said, 'I meant it.'" —Scott, 19

Reaction: "How am I supposed to deal with this? Everyone will talk about us or think it's my fault."

Possible response: "I know it's a lot to take in, but please remember that I'm the same person you loved 15 minutes ago. I haven't changed, you just know me better now. A lot of families have been in this situation. It might help for you to talk to some of them. PFLAG is a group for families of GLBTQ people. Here is the contact information for the local chapter. You don't have to call or go to their website right now, but I hope you'll at least take the information and know there are people out there you can talk to who won't judge you or us, or how you're feeling about all of this."

BEEN THERE

"My older sister was awful when I came out to her. There were a lot of unprovoked screaming matches between the two of us for a couple of months. She eventually calmed down and is now totally accepting." —Maria, 19

Now What? After "The Talk"

Family dynamics can change a lot after someone comes out. Coming out can start arguments or, at the very least, spark a lot of questions. Will you want to bring a boyfriend or girlfriend over? Should you be allowed to have sleepovers? Should the rules that applied to friends of the opposite sex now apply to same-sex friends?

Coming out may be the end of your hiding something, but it's the beginning of relearning some of your family dynamics. The keys to dealing with these changes are patience and open communication. The questions don't have to be answered all at once. They can be addressed as you go along. Talk about the issues you're facing and try to come up with solutions together. You might find that coming out ends up bringing your family closer together.

After the coming out conversation, some family members might act like you never told them. They could be hoping it will go away. They might be going through denial. Parents, for example, often struggle with shock, denial, and guilt when a son or daughter first comes out to them. They might hope that you're only going through a phase, or they might feel guilty that there was something they did that somehow caused you to be GLBTQ.

Remember that coming out is a process for all involved. Give your family time, but don't assume no news is good news and everyone is dealing with it. It's good to check in now and then. Mention to family members that you're there and willing to talk to them if they have questions or issues they want to discuss. They might need your help coping with this change. Continue to encourage (not demand) that they get in touch with others who have GLBTQ family members. If they do want to talk with you, try to keep conversations civil and productive. These discussions can get pretty heated, but take a deep breath (or several) and try to relate to what they might be going through.

A Place for Support

TrevorSpace
(www.trevorspace.org).
TrevorSpace is a social networking site where young people ages 13 to 24 can connect with and support one another. TrevorSpace is carefully monitored by administrators designated by The Trevor Project, a national organization focused on crisis and suicide prevention among GLBTQ teens. The forum provides accurate information that is age-appropriate and teen-friendly.

Chicas, Peeps, and Brahs: Coming Out to Your Friends

Like a lot of young people, you might choose to come out to a friend, or many friends, before you tell adults at home. It's not surprising that a lot of teens come out to friends first. After all, they're usually the people you have the most in common with. You might feel you'll get the best reaction from them.

Just like coming out to parents, coming out to friends can lead to a variety of reactions. Some friends might be supportive, some confused, some upset, and some might have a combination of these and other feelings. Some friends might even come out to you!

BEEN THERE
"So far, I have only come out to one friend — my best friend — and that was only after he told me that he was bi. It was funny. We were just sitting there and all of a sudden he says, 'I like guys. But I like girls, too.' Then I said, 'Me, too!' It was that simple, and we talk about it all the time now." — Alejandro, 19

Coming out to friends first can be great. If they're supportive, they can be there for you if you come out to your family. But just like with adults at home, consider all angles before coming out. If a friend is upset by the news, she might tell other people, which could be bad if you're trying to be selective about who knows.

As with parents and other family adults, it's a good idea to test the waters by gauging your friend's attitudes toward GLBTQ people. Some friends are more mature or may have had more experience dealing with GLBTQ issues. Maybe they have other queer friends or family members.

If you do decide to come out to a friend, follow the same steps you would with family members. In other words: prepare and be patient. It's important to remember that if your friend doesn't react well, it could be because he's heard negative things about GLBTQ people. Talk with him about what he thinks and why. Assure him that you're still the same person you've always been and you're still his friend—being queer doesn't change that.

Coming out can change your friendships. You could become closer than ever. Or your friend could be hurt that you didn't tell him before. He could be concerned that you're attracted to him, or he might even worry that if you're queer, maybe he is, too.

BEEN THERE

"I was lucky enough to have my closest friends be open and accepting. There were those other 'friends' who rejected me, but the ones I called my best friends kept their arms open to me. I think a lot of people act homophobic because they are scared of what people think. I think that if a friend — a truly great friend — were to find out that you are gay, they will love you for who you are."
—Lily, 20

"When you come out to friends — even if you're scared and nervous — don't act like it. Tell them you're GLBTQ with confidence. If they see you are confident, they will be confident in you and your friendship." —Paulo, 19

Again, give your friend time to adjust. Make it clear that you're ready to talk whenever he is. Some friendships do end because one person comes out, but these are extreme cases. Let your friend know that one of the reasons you told him is that you want to be honest with him about who you are. Tell him, too, that you're going to need his support to deal with people who aren't as accepting. Even if he's upset at first, chances are things will get better. And who knows, he might even surprise you by telling you he'd already figured out on his own that you're queer!

Coming Out at School

Some teens feel safer or more comfortable coming out to a trusted teacher, school counselor, or administrator. Some come out as a means of reaching out for support or guidance, or to get help dealing with harassment that's taking place at school. This might be true for you as well.

Adults who aren't family members can be good advocates and help you deal with issues you're facing. It's important to remember that teachers and other school officials are people just like everyone else—you can never be absolutely certain how they'll react. But because they aren't family, your coming out is less likely to trigger some of the more extreme emotions people at home might feel.

Some schools' policies make it difficult for supportive teachers to be vocal about their acceptance of GLBTQ people. But it's not uncommon for teachers who are supportive to let students know, in subtle or more obvious ways, their feelings. If your school has a gay-straight alliance, the group probably has a faculty or staff advisor. If that teacher is approachable, she could be a good person for you to talk with when you need the advice and support of an adult. Gradually, more teachers also are starting to come out at school. These GLBTQ teachers can be good sources of support.

BEEN THERE

"In my last year of junior high, I had this amazing Personal Development and Relationships teacher who I think was a lesbian. She taught us about being homosexual and bisexual. I think it was in that class that I actually discovered the term for what I was." — Iris, 19

School counselors are trained to talk with teens about challenges, and many of them can be very helpful. Unfortunately, some of them might also be homophobic. School counselors are sometimes, but not always, bound by confidentiality. This means they can't share what you say to them with anyone else—it has to be kept in confidence. In some cases, there is no confidentiality requirement. Some schools even require counselors to report certain things to the administration.

Counselors can be great people to seek advice and support from. If you're worried about talking to a counselor because of confidentiality issues, check your student handbook. The school's policy toward confidentiality should appear there. If you don't have a copy of the handbook, one should be available from the administrative office or at the school's website.

As students and advocacy groups work to make schools safer, more accepting places for GLBTQ teens, teachers and staff are learning what it means to be GLBTQ and are better able to understand and support queer students.

Chapter 4
Life at School

I can't even think straight.

One of the most challenging parts of being a GLBTQ teen can be coping with life at school. You have social hierarchies and cliques, teachers piling on the homework, administrators watching your every move, and teammates who are counting on you. Meanwhile, you're going through the normal stages of adolescence, which may have you feeling anything *but* normal. It's common to have times when you don't feel like you belong in your own skin. And on top of all that, you're coming to terms with possibly being queer.

School Life for GLBTQ Teens: The Big Picture

Surveys have revealed that life at school can range from pretty uncomfortable to downright dangerous for GLBTQ teens. The Gay, Lesbian and Straight Education Network's (GLSEN) "2009 National School Climate Survey"—the most comprehensive report on the experiences of lesbian, gay, bisexual, and transgender students—surveyed 7,261 students between the ages of 13 and 21.

Among the findings were the following:

- 85 percent of GLBTQ teens had experienced harassment in the past year
- 40 percent reported being physically harassed (such as being physically blocked from walking down the hall) and 19 percent reported being physically assaulted (punched, kicked, etc.) at school in the past year because of their sexual orientation
- 89 percent heard the word "gay" used in a negative way frequently or often at school; 72 percent heard derogatory remarks such as "faggot" or "dyke" frequently or often at school
- 62 percent of students who were harassed or assaulted in school did not report incidents to school staff because they believed little or no action would be taken and that the situation could become worse if they reported it
- 34 percent of students who reported incidents of harassment said that school staff did nothing in response
- More than half (53 percent) of students reported being harassed or threatened via electronic media such as text messages, emails, instant messages, or postings on social networking sites (also known as *cyberbullying*)
- 61 percent of students reported that they felt unsafe in school because of their sexual orientation, and more than 40 percent felt unsafe because of their gender expression
- The reported grade point average of students who were more frequently harassed because of their sexual orientation or gender expression was almost half a grade lower than for students who were harassed less often
- Only 18 percent of respondents attended a school that had a comprehensive safe school policy that specifically mentioned sexual orientation, gender identity, and/or gender expression
- Only 15 states and the District of Columbia have comprehensive anti-bullying/harassment laws that include sexual orientation, gender identity, and/or gender expression

On a more positive note, GLSEN also found that the number of sources of support for GLBTQ teens is growing, including gay-straight alliances (GSAs). A GSA is a student-led school club that aims to create a safe, welcoming, accepting school environment for all students—regardless of their sexual orientation or gender identity.

GLSEN's research shows that students in schools with a GSA reported hearing fewer homophobic remarks and experienced less harassment and assault because of their sexual orientation and gender expression (the way a person dresses or acts in relation to her or his gender identity). Students at these schools were also less likely to feel unsafe because of their orientation or gender expression, and they were more likely to tell school staff if they'd been harassed or assaulted. More information on GSAs, including suggestions for starting one in your school, can be found beginning on page 79.

The research also showed that having a safe school policy that includes sexual orientation and/or gender identity and expression makes a difference. Students at these schools heard fewer homophobic remarks and were less frequently victimized because of their sexual orientation. Staff members at these schools were also more likely to intervene when hearing homophobic remarks. Improvements in climate were also seen in schools where staff members are knowledgeable about GLBTQ issues and the curriculum is queer-inclusive.

Feeling Invisible . . . or *Too* Visible

Feeling invisible is something that most GLBTQ people experience at one time or another, regardless of age. It's difficult to grow up not seeing many positive representations of people like you. You might sometimes feel like you're the only one. Living in a predominantly straight society can be very isolating at times.

Is Anybody Else Out There?

As you walk through the cafeteria, the air is buzzing with girls talking about boys and boys talking about girls. And then there's you, who might be interested in boys, or girls, or both, or neither. In situations like this, it's easy to feel like a square peg in a round hole.

Visibility can be a problem not only in the cafeteria, but also in the curriculum. Debates are taking place all across the country about whether GLBTQ topics should be included in what you learn at school. While some schools do allow and encourage teachers to integrate these subjects into the curriculum, many others do not. In some districts, teachers can even be disciplined for mentioning queerness. If your classes don't include any mention of GLBTQ people, it can seem like you just appeared out of nowhere.

It can help to remember a lot of GLBTQ teens are out there. Many of them are going through situations and issues similar to your own. You're not "abnormal," and you're definitely not alone.

BEEN THERE

"In high school, the fact that I was aware of my differentness made my experience difficult. Coming out created a situation that didn't allow me to shy away from my reality. By the time I graduated, I had a fairly good idea of what to expect from others and myself."
—Adrian, 20

Four Ways to Fight Feeling Invisible

Here are some positive things you can do to keep from feeling isolated:

1. Research your GLBTQ "roots." The next time you're assigned a project for which you can choose your own topic, think about researching some of your queer predecessors. Write about poet Walt Whitman, painter Georgia O'Keefe, composer Peter Tchaikovsky, singer Bessie Smith, or professional tennis player Dr. Renee Richards. Offer a history lesson on the Stonewall uprising and how it shaped the GLBTQ rights movement or a political science presentation on the debate over queer marriage rights. Learn about the people who came before you, their challenges and their triumphs. It can help you appreciate what a long and rich history queer people have.

2. Get in touch with other GLBTQ teens. You might meet people at local GLBTQ organizations, online, or through others you know. (Chapter 5, beginning on page 85, has more information about meeting others.) It's important to talk with people who understand what you're going through and who can support you. Plus, it can be satisfying when you can support someone else in return.

3. Get involved in creating change. You might join or start a GSA at your school. You could also get involved with a local or national GLBTQ group. Being an activist is a great way to meet people with common interests, and it feels good to work for something positive.

4. Give yourself opportunities to shine. Take part in activities that give you a chance to feel good about yourself—maybe even show off a little. These don't have to be GLBTQ-related. If you're a great singer, try out for that solo in the spring concert. Take an art class and paint your heart out. Enter an amazing project in the science fair. Show off your speed on the track team. Dust off your guitar and start a band. Give yourself opportunities to succeed and enjoy yourself.

I Wish I Could Just Blend In

Maybe the problem is that you feel *too* visible. If you're subjected to taunts and harassment or bullying much of the day, a little invisibility might seem like a good thing. A lot of GLBTQ teens probably share those feelings. Remember those statistics from the GLSEN survey at the beginning of this chapter? You're not alone.

Even if you decide to come out voluntarily, the amount of attention it brings could be unexpected and overwhelming (although that's not always the case). You can reach out for help and find ways to make that visibility less scary by getting involved in a GSA or working to change your school environment. And you do have friends among your straight peers, whether you're aware of it yet or not. As our society

It Gets Better Project
Concerned that being queer will mean you're never accepted by others? Check out this website (www.itgetsbetterproject.com) to find inspiring messages from queer young people, GLBTQ adults, straight allies, and celebrities. The video archive shows many people who accept you for who you are.

becomes more educated about what it means to be queer, more and more of our straight allies are realizing 1) we're really not so different, and 2) we need their visible support when it comes to standing up for our rights as human beings.

BEEN THERE

"I think the hardest part of being out at school was the social aspect. All of my friends were very supportive. However, seeing the reactions of many of my classmates was extremely disheartening. Seeing that people found it entirely logical to hate me without knowing me not only hurt, but also made me lose a lot of faith in people. I wondered, 'If these misunderstandings and beliefs are so difficult for people to see through or question, what else could be entirely misunderstood? What may I need to take a closer look at or question?' And that's what sparked me to really search for what I thought, not what I was told to think or what everyone else thought — politically, spiritually, socially, and personally. I have become a much more satisfied, fulfilled, and confident person as a result." — Owen, 19

"Being a lesbian, or even being perceived as one, had its constraints in high school. I was always pretty guarded. My life was school and softball and work. Then I started to date someone who went to the same school and the lid blew off, but no one was saying anything. That, I think, was the worst thing for me. I was being closely watched and no one would say why. But since then, it seems that half the student population felt a need to come out. Sometimes I think I had something to do with that." — Davina, 20

Exercising Your Rights as a GLBTQ Student

Some schools have policies that protect students from bullying and harassment based on sexual orientation and gender identity. Your school's harassment policy (it may be called a "safe schools policy") usually can be found in your student handbook. Even if your school doesn't include sexual orientation and gender identity in its policy on bullying and harassment, you still have a right as a human being to be safe at school. Administrators and teachers are legally responsible for protecting all students. And you have options for how to deal with harassment.

Teen Heroes:
Changing the Environment for Queer Students

Sometimes it's difficult to believe that one person can make a big difference, but you can make a difference. And what's more, you're *not* alone in the fight against discrimination and harassment. Other teens, just like you, are engaged in similar struggles. And many adults and straight peers are willing to help. You *can* make a difference by standing up against prejudice and asking others to do the same.

Take a look at how some of these teens fought harassment in their schools.

Jacob Sullivan. In 2009, 14-year-old Jacob Sullivan, with the help of the New York Civil Liberties Union, filed suit against the Mohawk Central School District. Jacob alleged that the district failed to protect him against ongoing harassment, physical abuse, and threats made against him due to his sexual orientation and nonconformity to masculine stereotypes. The U.S. Justice Department later joined the suit, which meant that this case could set a precedent for future rulings and involve a broader interpretation of a federal law prohibiting gender discrimination.

The suit was settled March 29, 2010, and, as part of the agreement, Jacob's family received $50,000. But perhaps more important, the district agreed to make its schools safer for students. It enlisted the support of the Anti-Defamation League and began training staff on how to better address issues of harassment. The school district also reviewed its policies on harassment based on sex, gender identity, gender expression, and sexual orientation in an effort to create a more positive atmosphere for all students.

Nick Garafola. In 2009, after surviving nearly relentless taunting that culminated in a physical altercation, Nick Garafola decided something needed to be done at his school. With the help of some interested peers and an adult advisor, Nick cofounded Spectrum, his school's gay-straight alliance. "We are currently working on a schoolwide beautification project, which will introduce GLBTQ-themed art into the building," Nick wrote in a 2009 article. "Mostly, though, our GSA is a fun and safe place for a bunch of us like-minded students to chill out and talk about homophobia and the differences between tolerating and embracing diversity."

Nick also created a Safe Zone program at his school. "The purpose of the Safe Zone program is to give all students—gay, lesbian, heterosexual, bisexual, questioning, or transgender—someone to talk to about sexual orientation and gender. . . . My mission is to create an environment of acceptance in which all students and teachers can take part." At Nick's school, a pink triangle is placed on the classroom doors of faculty members who have designated themselves as "allies." These allies are

▼ **National Day of Silence** The National Day of Silence brings attention to anti-GLBTQ name-calling, bullying, and harassment in schools. Participants take a vow of silence for part or all of the school day and often hand out "speaking cards" that explain their silence and educate others about issues facing GLBTQ teens.

The National Day of Silence has become the largest student-led action promoting safer schools for all, regardless of sexual orientation, gender identity, or gender expression. The project has grown from one event and 150 participants in 1996 to currently hundreds of thousands of students at more than 8,000 participating schools.

The following is text from an actual 2009 speaking card:

"Please understand my reasons for not speaking today. I am participating in the Day of Silence (DOS), a national youth movement bringing attention to the silence faced by lesbian, gay, bisexual, and transgender people and their allies. My deliberate silence echoes that silence, which is caused by anti-LGBT bullying, name-calling, and harassment. I believe that ending the silence is the first step toward building awareness and making a commitment to address these injustices. Think about the voices you are not hearing today."

For more information on the National Day of Silence, including organizing kits and news updates, visit the event website (www.dayofsilence.org). Another great resource for promoting GLBTQ-friendly learning environments is GLSEN's ThinkB4YouSpeak (www.thinkb4youspeak.com). Visit the site to learn how you can address the use of anti-queer language (words like "fag" and "dyke") in your school. ▼

taught about the issues teens face regarding sexual orientation and gender.

Dylan Theno. Dylan Theno isn't gay, but because he was perceived to be by some of his classmates, he was threatened and verbally harassed so much that he dropped out of school during his junior year. The harassment started when he was in seventh grade. Dylan brought a federal suit against the Tonganoxie School District in Kansas for failing to protect him. In 2005, he won a $440,000 settlement.

Joseph Ramelli and Megan Donovan. Joseph Ramelli and Megan Donovan, both gay, were repeatedly threatened and harassed by students at Poway High School (near San Diego, California). During their senior year, Joseph and Megan had to be homeschooled because of the harassment. The students filed a lawsuit and, in 2005, were awarded $300,000. The jury found that, even though school officials were aware of the harassment, they failed to protect Joseph and Megan.

Pat Doe. Fifteen-year-old transgender student known in court documents as Pat Doe took her school to court over her right to express her gender identity by wearing girls' clothing. According to GLBTQ magazine *The Advocate,* Pat's principal had deemed it "disruptive" for a biologically male student to wear "feminine" clothing. In 2000, a Massachusetts appellate court agreed with Pat and she returned to school able to dress as she felt comfortable.

Alana Flores. In 1997, Alana Flores was regularly harassed at her school in Morgan Hill, California. She repeatedly received death threats written on her locker, including the words, "Die, dyke bitch" and "We'll kill you." Alana took the threatening notes to the assistant principal, who dismissed her complaints and told her to go back to class.

In 1998, Alana and five other students sued the school district for repeatedly ignoring the reports they made about being harassed and bullied by others who thought they were gay. In 2004, the school district was ordered to pay $1.1 million in legal fees and damages. Schools in Morgan Hill also implemented a training program for teachers and administrators to try to eliminate anti-gay harassment. The case set the precedent by a federal court that schools aware of anti-gay harassment must take meaningful steps to stop it.

Jamie Nabozny. Jamie Nabozny suffered such violent abuse and harassment that he was forced to drop out of his Ashland, Wisconsin, high school. Jamie brought a lawsuit against the school district, and in 1996, a federal court ruled in his favor, stating that the school had failed to provide him with a safe learning environment. The school agreed to pay nearly $1 million to settle the case. The landmark decision—that schools can be held liable for deliberately ignoring anti-gay harassment—set a precedent for similar cases and forced many schools to examine their own policies. Jamie's story is featured in the documentary *Bullied* (see page 209).

According to the ACLU, since 1996 courts have awarded more than $4 million to gay, lesbian, bisexual, and transgender students who filed lawsuits against schools for refusing to take adequate steps to stop anti-queer harassment.

Filing a lawsuit may not be the best solution for every situation, but it is an option. As Nick Garafola showed, you can create change without going to court. But the results of these and

> **Legal Assistance**
> **Lambda Legal**
> (www.lambdalegal.org). This national organization works for the equality of people who are GLBTQ. With offices located throughout the country, Lambda Legal may be able to help you address injustices in your school. You can also reach the group by calling (212) 809-8585.
>
> **American Civil Liberties Union**
> (www.aclu.org). The American Civil Liberties Union (ACLU) has supported GLBTQ civil rights with legal aid since the 1960s. Visit the ACLU's website to learn about cases the group has pursued on behalf of queer students. You can also call (212) 549-2500 to report discrimination.

similar cases across the country have resulted in some schools voluntarily protecting GLBTQ students from harassment. Many teens see these rulings as evidence that they should not have to endure harassment, and they're right.

The Voice of Authority: Talking to Teachers and Administrators

Teachers, administrators, and other school officials can be some of your greatest allies, or they can be some of your biggest headaches.

For some students, even worse than bullying and harassment from other students is dealing with prejudice from school officials. According to Human Rights Watch, an international organization working for the equality of all people, many students find discrimination by teachers even more demoralizing and difficult to deal with than anything their peers say or do.

Some school officials and teachers harass teens by making anti-GLBTQ remarks. Some turn a blind eye to harassment by students or other members of the school community. Others tell GLBTQ students that it's their own fault because they invite harassment by "flaunting" who they are.

However it occurs, mistreatment by school staff is unacceptable. There are actions you can take to help make your school safer for everyone.

Confronting Authority

Here are some ways you can confront harassment and discrimination by officials or teachers at your school:

Action: Approach the offending official or teacher. Tell him how his speech or behavior makes you feel. Explain that when he ignores or participates in harassment, it sends a message to students that it's okay. Stay calm and rational as you talk to the person. This can be difficult, but it can help you make your point more effectively.

Action: Tell a parent, guardian, or another adult. Parents or guardians can be helpful allies in standing up to bullies, especially if the bullies are other adults. Confronting an adult can be very intimidating, so it's a good idea to have the support of at least one adult you trust.

Action: Tell an administrator. If the perpetrator of prejudice is a teacher or another staff member, report her to an administrator such as a principal or vice principal. If the perpetrator is an administrator herself, approach the school superintendent or the school board. If you're going that high up the chain of command, it's especially good to have an adult backup—a parent, a lawyer, someone from a national GLBTQ organization, or a combination of these.

On Your Side: Getting Support from School Staff

Many teachers and administrators want to help protect queer students from bullying and harassment. Some might speak up when they hear anti-GLBTQ language or see physical harassment. If your school has a GSA, the group's faculty advisor could also be a good advocate for you. Enlist the help of any official who you know wants to support queer students at school.

As with coming out, when it comes to bullying, it helps to be prepared before taking action. Get informed, know what your resources are, and get yourself in a solid, positive mindset.

1. Consult with a group such as GLSEN, the ACLU, or Lambda Legal to find out exactly what your legal rights are at school.
2. Research how students at other schools have had success in confronting issues with teachers or school administrators. You might be able to connect with some of these peers via email or an online social network.

BEEN THERE
"I actually found out that my math teacher was a lesbian. After I graduated we ended up becoming friends." —Jennifer, 18

3. Prepare your "case" with detailed notes, witnesses, and examples. Even if you're not going to court (at least, *not yet*) it's helpful to think of your situation as a case. Being detailed helps others see that you're serious.
4. Be calm and rational. If you're overly emotional, the authorities might try to dismiss you as overreacting.
5. Keep it simple. State your problem as briefly as you can and stick to the facts. Stay away from giving your personal opinions (unless you're asked), and provide a factual account of the events.

6. Listen. There are two sides to every story. It can be tough to listen to the person doing the bullying give his version of the story, but remember that acting calmly and rationally will help demonstrate your maturity and your seriousness about confronting the problem.

For more information on dealing with bullying, including cyberbullying, see page 35.

Club Life: Gay-Straight Alliances (GSAs) and Other Queer-Friendly Activities

Gay-straight alliances are student-led groups that work to create a safe, welcoming, accepting school environment for all students.

GSAs have received a lot of coverage in the media. Some school districts have attempted to block their formation, but your right to form a GSA in your school is protected by the law. There are two laws that apply—the First Amendment (protecting freedom of speech and assembly) and the federal Equal Access Act (providing for equal treatment of all non-instructional, student-initiated clubs). All over the country, students are fighting back and standing up for their rights to form GSAs.

Common Questions and Answers About GSAs

Here are some common questions and answers about gay-straight alliances. More information about GSAs is also available from GLSEN (www.glsen.org) and the GSA Network (www .gsanetwork.org).

Q: Who gets involved in gay-straight alliances?
A: GSAs welcome any student who feels that harassment and discrimination against GLBTQ people, their families, and their friends is wrong.

Q: How many GSAs are there?
A: Gay-straight alliances can be found in public, private, and parochial high schools and middle schools of various sizes all over the country. More than 4,000 GSAs are registered with GLSEN.

Q: Do people in gay-straight alliances talk about sex?
A: That's not the purpose of GSAs. These groups meet just like any other school club, but the activities range from discussions of gender roles or what it means to be queer to working on

projects aimed at making the school a safer space for GLBTQ students. GLSEN supports several events that many gay-straight alliances participate in. Among these are Ally Week in October, TransACTION! in November, Dr. Martin Luther King Jr. Organizing Weekend in January, and the National Day of Silence in April.

BEEN THERE

"I cofounded the GSA at my school. My friend and I wrote the appropriate letters and had meetings with the principal. We also found a faculty advisor, figured out a place to meet, chose our meeting time, and named our group. It was an uphill battle, during which we came head-to-head with the principal several times. But we managed to do some good things, like hold events for National Coming Out Day and the National Day of Silence. The group was definitely controversial, but we helped to raise a lot of awareness."
—Arian, 19

How to Start a GSA

If you're interested in starting a gay-straight alliance at your school, here are some basic steps to get things moving:

1. Find out and follow your school's guidelines. You establish a GSA the same way you would any other school club. Look in your student handbook for your school's rules for starting a group. You may find guidelines or a set process you need to follow (for example, writing a club mission statement).

2. Find a faculty advisor. Consider teachers or staff members who you think would be supportive or who have shown support for GLBTQ issues. Your school might have guidelines about who is eligible to be a club advisor.

3. Find other interested students. GSAs are for both GLBTQ and straight students. Straight students who feel that anti-GLBTQ discrimination is wrong are often strong and vocal GSA members. Look for members all over your school. The more diverse the GSA membership is, the stronger and more effective it can be.

4. Talk to the administration. Tell school officials what you're doing and try to get their support. If they're supportive, they can help the GSA gain acceptance among students, teachers, and the community. If administrators oppose the formation of the group, inform them (calmly and kindly) of your legal rights to start a club.

5. Pick a meeting place. Select a place in the school that affords some privacy, but is also easily accessible. It could be a classroom, counselor's office, or conference room.

6. Advertise. Let others know about the meeting through posters, flyers, a page on a social networking website, word-of-mouth, the school's website, and any other (appropriate) method you can think of. Some people may tear down or put graffiti on your flyers and posters. Don't be discouraged. Have a reserve stash so you can post more.

7. Plan an agenda. Think about what you want to do at your first meeting and plan ahead. You can do anything from holding discussions and playing get-to-know-you games to having a guest speaker and planning a workshop. Visit the websites of organizations that support GSAs for more meeting ideas.

▼ **The Official Ruling** U.S. District Court Judge David O. Carter made a landmark decision on GSAs. He stated in his ruling, "To the extent that the [school] board opens up its school facilities to any noncurriculum related group, it must open its facilities to all student groups."

Also, on August 5, 2010, Pennsylvania Senator Bob Casey, joined by 10 cosponsors, introduced the Safe Schools Improvement Act in the U.S. Senate. In 2009, California Representative Linda Sánchez introduced the bill in the House of Representatives, where it has 119 bipartisan cosponsors. The bill requires schools that receive funding under the Safe and Drug-Free Schools and Communities Act to implement a comprehensive anti-bullying policy that includes sexual orientation and gender identity/expression. It also requires states to include bullying and harassment data in statewide needs assessments reporting.

For more information about legal rights and GSAs, visit the websites of GLSEN (www.glsen.org) and the ACLU (www.aclu.org/safeschools). ▼

8. Hold the meeting. A good idea for the first meeting is to have members introduce themselves, discuss why the group is needed, plan your overall goals, and brainstorm projects for the year. You also might want to plan to elect group members for president, vice president, treasurer, and other club offices so that you have a leadership structure.

9. Set ground rules. At the first meeting, work together to create rules to ensure that discussions are safe, confidential, and respectful. Make sure group members know that everyone's views are welcome.

10. Plan for the future. Set goals for what you want the GSA to accomplish, not only in the next few months but also in the long term. Be realistic about what you can do over the course of the year, but don't limit yourself. You might be amazed at what you can achieve.

> ## The Birth of the GSA
> Did you know that the first gay-straight alliance was founded by a straight student? In 1988, a straight student at Concord Academy in Concord, Massachusetts, wanted to do something to help educate her fellow students about anti-queer bullying and harassment. She approached her history teacher—GLSEN founder Kevin Jennings—and proposed the idea for the club. A short time later, Jennings became the faculty advisor for the nation's first GSA. Now GSAs are in more than 1,000 schools across the United States. Each year, nearly 20,000 students are directly involved in GSA activities.

This information is adapted from GLSEN's "Jump-Start Guide to Building and Activating Your GSA."

Moving On:
Deciding If You Need to Change Schools

Unfortunately, some queer teens end up having to change schools because officials are unwilling to address bullying and harassment. Some may ignore or even participate in the mistreatment.

Making the Change

If you've explored all of your options for bringing an end to harassment—talking with teachers, administrators, school superintendents, the school board, and people from national GLBTQ organizations—and it hasn't worked, or if you believe you're in serious danger, it might be time to change schools. Approach your parent or guardian and talk with him or her about why you feel it's necessary for you to make the change.

Moving to a new school won't necessarily mean an end to bullying and harassment. You might still encounter problems similar to the ones you had at your previous school. It's a good idea to have your parent or guardian contact administrators at your new prospective school to find out their stance on GLBTQ harassment issues. If attitudes at your new school aren't any better (or are even worse) than your current school, it might be wise to look at other options. You could consider getting legal assistance from a national GLBTQ or civil rights organization. Homeschooling or studying for the GED at a local community college are other possibilities. A few large cities (including New York, Los Angeles, Dallas, and Milwaukee) even have schools— public and private—specifically for queer students.

▼ **An Online School for Queer Teens** In 2010, GLBTQ Online High School opened its virtual doors to its first students. The school is the world's first online high school created specifically for gay, lesbian, bisexual, and transgender teens, or teens questioning their sexuality or gender. The school provides an interactive online education, complete with highly qualified teachers in all of the subject areas you'd find at brick-and-mortar high schools, and a few more, such as queer studies. GLBTQ Online High School also provides extensive adult and peer support, as well as one-on-one support from counselors specially trained in GLBTQ issues among young people. Students can enroll on a full- or part-time basis, and some scholarships are available. For more information about the school, visit www.glbtqonlinehighschool.com. ▼

Staying in School

Whatever you do, continue your education. GLBTQ teens often have much higher absenteeism and dropout rates than their straight peers. According to "The 2009 National School Climate Survey," 29 percent of GLBTQ students missed a class and 30 percent missed an entire day of school in the past month because of feeling unsafe, compared to only 8 percent and 7 percent, respectively, of a national sample of secondary school students. Also, queer students who experience harassment often get lower grades than their straight peers and may disengage from school altogether. Queer teens were more likely to report that they didn't plan to pursue any post-secondary education (or getting a high school diploma or finishing high school at all) than their straight peers.

BEEN THERE

"I dropped out of high school after six months of constant torture. Being gay, or being perceived to be gay, affected me very negatively, to the point of being suicidal, because of all the daily harassment. (Now I'm being homeschooled.) But I've found that being gay has opened up so many doors for me. My life would be so incredibly different if I weren't gay. Every once in a while I will think about what my life would have been like if I'd been straight, and well, I don't think that I would be as happy as I am right now. I mean, why would I want to be anyone other than who I am?" —Robert, 15

An education is incredibly important, and although it might seem like a good solution at the time, dropping out of school will seriously limit your future opportunities. Don't let a group of ignorant people rob you of your future. Whether you change schools, homeschool, get your GED, attend school online, or opt for early college admission, getting an education is your ticket to the life you want and deserve.

Chapter 5
GLBTQ Friends

We are family.

If being GLBTQ is normal and queer people aren't all that different from straight people, why should it matter if you have GLBTQ friends?

If you're out and have close straight friends, that's great. And if your immediate or extended family members have been supportive, that's great, too. At the same time, it can help to know people who really understand what it's like to be queer. For some GLBTQ people, it isn't until they are able to spend time with other queer people that they truly feel part of a peer group.

For many teens, their most influential role models are family members. But in most cases, GLBTQ teens can't be *just* like their mom or dad, a grandparent, or an aunt or uncle because odds are these people are straight. A lot of queer teens haven't grown up with role models or friends they can truly identify with. Having queer friends can help these GLBTQ teens feel more comfortable with their sexual orientation or gender identity.

BEEN THERE

"During high school, I got involved with a GLBTQ counseling/social group. I loved it. It really helped me feel more comfortable with myself. All the other kids who went there were from different schools. It was nice because it was like forming our own little community. Every week after the 'session,' which we just called 'group,' we'd go out to eat. We had so much fun." —Valencia, 19

"It's like being in your own private club. It's like having an inside joke that not everyone understands. But when you do find someone who understands, there is an immediate connection that goes beyond words and finds itself in common experiences." —Walt, 20

Part of the Family: The Utterly Diverse, Somewhat Cohesive, Always Interesting GLBTQ Community

One of the best things about being GLBTQ is the sense of community you can feel with other queer people. In fact, one of the ways some GLBTQ identify one another is by using the word "family." As in, "You know Tyree, the guy in our chem class? He's family." Some people even have bumper stickers that read "Family" or "Family car."

Just like any family, though, we don't always get along. So you can't assume that all GLBTQ people will like or even tolerate each other. Although we're part of a larger group, we're individuals with our own personalities and histories. Being GLBTQ is a major characteristic to have in common, but it might also be the *only* thing you have in common.

At first you might feel intimidated by the GLBTQ community. You might worry about not being "queer enough" or not following the "GLBTQ rules." You'll soon discover, however, that the GLBTQ community is as diverse as people can be. Whether you're a drama queen, a jock, a butch, a femme, a gender bender, a girlie girl, a manly man, a transman, a club kid, a prep, an urban hipster, a country boy, an androgyne, a hip-hop head, a surfer dude, a hippie chick, none of the above, or even several of the above, there's room for you just as you are.

IMRU2? Meeting Other GLBTQ Teens

Throughout history, queer people have come up with some pretty creative secret ways to identify each other. In the past, one gay man might have approached another man and asked, "Are you a friend of Dorothy?" If the man answered, "yes," that meant he was also gay. This phrase, which was a reference to Dorothy in *The Wizard of Oz,* is just one example of the many ways GLBTQ people have devised to discreetly identify one another. If you ever come across a T-shirt or sticker that reads "Friend of Dorothy," now you're in the know.

Great Places to Meet Other GLBTQ Teens

Regardless of whether you believe in gaydar (see the sidebar on this page), here are some tips that can help you find other GLBTQ teens.

Gaydar

Hey, what's that beeping? Did you know that the word *gaydar* is now in the dictionary? *Merriam-Webster's* dictionary defines gaydar as "the ability to recognize homosexuals through observation or intuition." Gaydar is short for "gay radar." Does gaydar really exist? Some people swear by it, but others have never heard a beep. You can decide for yourself.

Queer community centers and organizations. GLBTQ groups sponsor programs that offer everything from social activities (like movie nights) to counseling services or homework help. These groups should be listed in your local telephone directory, or you can search the Internet using keywords like "gay community center" along with your city and state. Centerlink (www.lgbtcenters.org) serves as an online directory for GLBTQ centers. The National Youth Advocacy Coalition, through a partnership with The Trevor Project, also provides info on state and local organizations working with GLBTQ teens (www .thetrevorproject.org/youth/local-resources).

BEEN THERE

"Even though I love my straight friends, it was a huge relief to meet other gay teens. It's nice to have people who totally understand what you're talking about, what it's like to come out, and all of that."
— Elizabeth, 17

GLBTQ bookstores. Go to a reading or just show up and casually flip through some periodicals. You could bump into other young people. If there's no GLBTQ bookstore in your area, there could be a queer section in your local bookstore.

Coffeehouses or other places where teens and students like to hang out. This strategy for meeting other queer teens may work especially well if your town has a gay neighborhood. Visiting a "gayborhood" can be a great way to work yourself into your community's GLBTQ scene without having to put yourself out there too much.

Speaking of Books . . . Finding Yourself in Literature

Just as it's important to connect with other GLBTQ people in real life, it's also great to see yourself represented in books. Being able to read about people (real or fictional) who are like you or who have had similar experiences is important to feeling "normal." Writer and blogger Lee Wind operates an award-winning site (www.leewind.org) for which he reviews and catalogs many books with GLBTQ characters and themes.

Underage clubs. Not all nightclubs are for those who are over 21. Many towns have underage clubs where teens can watch live music, play games, or just hang out. Going to these places can help increase your chances of meeting GLBTQ people your own age.

▼ A Note About the Club Scene

Some young people, desperate to meet or just be around other GLBTQ people, sneak in to gay clubs or other hangouts for people over 21. Sneaking into bars or clubs could spell trouble for you for a few reasons, not the least of which is it's illegal. You also risk being in situations you're not prepared for—underage drinking, drug use, smoking—even though you're just looking for friendship. The last thing you need is a big setback in your life by getting involved in the club scene where you could even get arrested. It's best to stick to activities and locations geared toward teens. That's also the best way to ensure you'll have opportunities to meet people your own age. ▼

How Do I Know If They're GLBTQ?

If you meet someone in a non-GLBTQ-centered place, it can be difficult to identify whether someone is queer. Even if your gaydar is beeping like crazy, try not to make any assumptions. Subtlety is usually the best tactic when trying to figure out if someone is GLBTQ. Regardless of how out you are, others might not take kindly to you waltzing up to them and asking, "You're queer, right?"

Here are some subtle strategies for figuring out if the person who caught your eye was actually winking or just trying to get rid of a loose eyelash.

- Start a conversation and reference something you saw on *Glee, The Ellen DeGeneres Show,* or if you're feeling bold, maybe even *RuPaul's Drag Race* or another show with queer people or characters in starring roles. Maybe he'll get the hint and drop his own.

- If you don't mind outing yourself, casually mention something about an ex-boyfriend or ex-girlfriend. For example, if you're in a coffee shop, say, "Hi, I noticed you sitting here by yourself. My ex was supposed to meet me here, but something must have come up because I don't see him/her. Mind if I share your table?"

- If you're at a bookstore, bring over a copy of a queer-themed book. Tell the person you're thinking about buying it and ask if she has heard anything about it. It doesn't win the subtle award, but it will probably help get the information you're looking for.

- If you're the straightforward type, go ahead and ask. But there's no need to shout, "Hey, are you queer?" At least start a conversation first and then slip it in. Think of how you might feel if someone walked up to you demanding to know your sexual orientation or gender identity. Keep in mind that if the person is straight, depending on his attitude, he might be offended by your question. Be prepared for a variety of responses.

Making Connections: GLBTQ Online Communities

The Internet is a great place to meet and talk with others. Whether you're an experienced surfer or you've barely gotten your feet wet, finding others online is easy.

Many websites sponsor scheduled chats, guest speakers and webinars, bulletin boards, and blogs. Some also allow you to have your own email account. You can chat online with other GLBTQ teens, post questions or conversation topics, talk to counselors, and so on.

It might take some trial and error to find what you're looking for online. You might end up visiting several sites before you settle on one, or a few, that you want to explore further.

BEEN THERE

"I've come out to people online, in large groups and in chat rooms, which is so much easier than in person or one-on-one." —Fatema, 19

The Internet: Stay Safe as You Surf

The Internet has grown exponentially in terms of its content and variety of websites. Unfortunately, the risks and number of people out there using the Web to victimize people—including GLBTQ teens—have also grown. Here are some things to think about when you're visiting a site:

Who sponsors the site? Could the site have an ulterior motive that could influence the content? One common motive is to sell you something. If you use a search engine to locate sites of interest to queer teens, it's common to find many that are actually selling subscriptions to dating and other social networking services. Some sites masquerade as youth help sites, but they are actually sponsored by religious groups or other organizations whose missions are to "convert" GLBTQ people.

Who's giving that advice? Keep in mind that at some sites, and especially bulletin boards, you don't know who is answering you or how valid the information is. It's a good idea to save serious questions for sites where counselors or experts provide information.

What kind of information do they want from you? Some sites require you to register before using them. Be wary of sites that require you to give information beyond a user name and a password. *And never give out your address or your phone number.*

Who are you talking to? You can never be absolutely sure who you're talking to online, so be careful and make decisions about what you say accordingly. Don't give out personal information like your phone number or where you live. It can be surprisingly easy to mention personal information in conversation without thinking about it. Typing something as simple as, "My little sis, Sarah, is scared because there's a huge storm brewing here in Little Creek," tells others where you live and that you have a younger sister, as well as her name. That might seem harmless, but someone with bad intentions could be looking for that type of information.

Meeting someone you became acquainted with online could be extremely dangerous. Your new friend could be exactly who he says he is—or he might not be. It's important to wait to meet someone you've met online until you can be accompanied by a family adult or another adult you trust.

Be *very* wary of anyone who requests a photo, especially if they ask for it right away, and *never* send a revealing photo. It's just not safe, and it's definitely not smart. You never know where the picture will show up, but it's a good bet that the person you send it to won't be the only one who sees it. Once it's out there,

▼ Some Places to Start on the Web

TrevorSpace (www.trevorspace.org). This is a social networking community for GLBTQ teens ages 13 to 24. What sets TrevorSpace apart from other social networking sites is that it's monitored by adults who are part of The Trevor Project, so it's a safe space for queer youth.

Amplify Your Voice (www.amplifyyourvoice.org/youthresource). GLBTQ teens can visit here for monthly features, message boards, and online peer education on topics including activism, culture, and sexual health.

GLSEN (www.glsen.org). This site is geared more toward activism-minded youth, but it's still a great place to get in touch with other teens. The organization can connect you with local chapters and GSAs, as well as other gay student groups. ▼

there's no getting it back. The same applies to sending sexually suggestive or explicit emails or text messages (often called "sexting"). It might seem like a fun idea at the time, but keep in mind that those messages can easily be saved and forwarded (and often are).

When chatting online, ditch anyone who uses inappropriate, suggestive, or coercive language—you don't need to waste your time on people who make you uncomfortable, speak to you disrespectfully, or attempt to manipulate you.

Queer Compadres: GLBTQ Friendships

Be yourself. As you're looking for GLBTQ friends, keep in mind that not just any queer person will do. As with all friendships, you need to be true to yourself. It's great to be friends with other GLBTQ people, as long as they're people you would pick to be your friends otherwise.

Don't waste your time on people who try to talk you into doing negative things, like using drugs and alcohol, just because they're GLBTQ. Queer people are just like anyone else—everyone is different. You'll like some and you won't like others. But don't lower your standards just to make friends. Knowing who you are and sticking to your beliefs can ensure you won't become involved in unhealthy relationships or activities.

Thinking about all of this could have you feeling like it's the first day of school all over again. Try not to worry, you'll make some good friends. Just to prove it, here are five reasons why:

1. You're true to your beliefs.
2. You're proud of who you are (or at least you're working on it).
3. You respect others' opinions.
4. You have a lot to offer.
5. You know that life can be very serious, but there's still a lot of room for fun.

BEEN THERE

"My senior year I realized I was living for myself and no one else. I had no one to please but me. I hung out with the people I wanted to and didn't worry about people other than that. I did the things I wanted to do and spoke my mind whether or not someone else agreed with it." —Emily, 18

Straight But Not Narrow: Other Friends

Straight friendships are no less valuable than GLBTQ ones. In fact, it's good to be friends with a wide variety of people. Exposure to different viewpoints helps make you a well-rounded, considerate person.

"That's soooo gay! Um, no offense."

It can be easy to become frustrated with some of your straight friends if they make remarks that you feel are insensitive or ignorant. But try to be patient with them. Bring remarks to their attention and calmly explain why they hurt your feelings or upset you. Many times you'll find that it's just a misunderstanding and your friend didn't realize how what she said sounded, or she thoughtlessly said something out of habit, or she didn't think it would be offensive. We all have things we can learn from each other. Give her a chance. You might be the first GLBTQ person she knows.

However, if you have a friend who is repeatedly offensive or even abusive and who doesn't care whether you're offended, you might want to rethink the friendship. GLBTQ or straight, do you really want to be friends with someone who treats you or anyone else like that?

Bridging the Gap

After you come out to a straight friend, he might feel uncomfortable (or he might be completely cool with it). Maybe he's still getting used to it and isn't exactly sure what your coming out to him means. Does it mean you're going to start dressing, acting, or talking in a different way? Will you still want to be friends or will you want new GLBTQ ones instead? Does it mean you want to date him?

These questions might come up right away, down the road, or not at all. But take time to address them if they do come up, because it will make your friendship stronger. Also, knowledge is contagious. The next time your friend hears someone demeaning GLBTQ people, he just might intervene. And that's how people and society start to change for the better.

Chapter 6

Dating and Relationships

I'm not a lesbian, but my girlfriend is.

Depending on where you live, the dating scene for GLBTQ teens may be quite happening—or it may seem like it's *not* happening. But regardless of whether you're in an urban, a suburban, or even a rural area, options do exist. Maybe your town doesn't hold events like queer proms, but GLBTQ teens still find ways to get together and have fun. As you become more comfortable with your sexuality, you might even start dating a little . . . or maybe a lot. The important thing to remember: whether you're experienced with dating, just beginning, or only starting to think about it, you decide how to run your love life.

Soul Searching:
Figuring Out If You're Ready to Date

When you're a teen, there can be a lot of pressure to date. But not everyone is ready. It all depends on where you are mentally and emotionally, and no two people are the same in that regard. If you're still trying to figure out who you are, it can be difficult to try to start a relationship with someone else. Still, for all teens—gay and straight—dating can be a normal and healthy part of developing positive personal relationships with others.

Trying to Fit In

Dating can be a lot of fun, but it can also feel like torture if you don't feel free to date the people you're really interested in. Many queer people end up in straight relationships or dating situations because they feel it's expected of them. Some may be attempting to fit in or trying to change their feelings of being queer.

It's common for GLBTQ teens to try to change or fit in. Some teens date people of the opposite sex in an attempt to hide their sexual orientation or in the hopes that it will make them heterosexual. Some even engage in heterosexual sex to try to deny their true identities.

If you find yourself in a situation where you're doing something that doesn't feel right, ask yourself if you're dating contrary to your wants and needs because you feel like you have to. If it's making you unhappy, you don't have to go on these dates. If, on the other hand, these dates are more about friends hanging out, then it's okay. The key is to be true to yourself and honest with the person you're spending time with.

Dating to Figure Things Out

If you're questioning, dating might be a positive way for you to explore your sexual orientation. You can meet new people, have some fun, and figure some things out. But while dating can help you answer some questions, sex won't. Engaging in sexual activity for the purpose of figuring out who you are is a bad idea, and it's not necessary. Being GLBTQ is about a lot more than who you sleep with. It's about your personal identity, so you don't need to have sex to become certain of your sexual orientation.

And you don't even have to date. If you're really feeling conflicted about your identity, the thought of dating might not appeal to you right now. The important thing is to listen to yourself. Don't do anything you're not ready for, because if you push yourself, things will just become more stressful. Remember, everything will sort itself out if you give it (and yourself) a chance.

> **The No-Holds-Barred Bare Naked Truth**
> You don't have to have sex to figure out your sexuality, sexual orientation, or gender identity. Period. Exclamation point.

Am I Ready? Dating Checklist

This checklist can help you figure out if you're ready. So, before you check out the dating scene, be sure to check off each of these items:

☑ I'm confident in myself.

☑ I don't feel like I need someone else's approval, and I don't feel the need to please others to the detriment of myself.

☑ I'm confident I can say "no" if someone pressures me to do something I don't want to do or am not sure about.

☑ I can be respectful of others' feelings and beliefs and won't try to force them to do something they're not comfortable with.

☑ If things don't work out with one person, I know plenty of others are out there.

Who Gets the Check? GLBTQ Dating Basics

Most of us get our ideas about romance from movies and TV, and there aren't that many examples of Lance sweeping Hector off his feet and living happily ever after, or of LaTisha and Gabrielle waltzing off into the sunset (although there are a lot more than there used to be). When queer relationships are shown, sometimes they're amplified versions of unhealthy relationship patterns. The lack of positive GLBTQ dating role models can make some teens nervous about the idea of dating.

Queer Dating Q&A

It's natural to have a lot of questions and some confusion as you enter the queer dating scene. Most likely, a lot of what you've learned is probably modeled after boy-girl dating. So what happens if it's boy-boy or girl-girl? Here are some common questions and answers:

Q: What's a GLBTQ relationship supposed to be like? How do I know what to do if we're both boys/girls?
A: What's any relationship supposed to be like? Starting to date is a confusing time for everyone, but it might feel a lot more confusing if you're GLBTQ. A lot of our behavior is based on long-held ideas about female and male roles in relationships. Being GLBTQ is a great opportunity to throw those stereotypes out the window and just be yourself. Let the personalities of you and the other person dictate what the relationship is like. As long as you're true to yourself and the relationship is healthy, you're off to a good start.

BEEN THERE
"The best thing about my boyfriend is that I don't feel like I have to worry what he'll think about anything. We're just cool with each other, and that's the most amazing feeling — when someone likes you just how you are." — Troy, 17

Q: How do I figure out who should pay?
A: More and more people are going Dutch—each person pays for his or her share. Many teens don't have a lot of pocket money to start with, so it helps if you split the tab. If only one person is going to pay, it's usually the person who initiated the date. But who says dates have to cost a lot of money? See the next answer for some cheap or free options.

Q: Where is a good place to go on a date?
A: The standards are dinner, a movie, or someplace like a coffee shop, mall, or arcade where you can hang out. Nothing wrong with those—they're classics. GLBTQ-friendly places like social events at queer community centers and underage clubs are great though, too, because you can be yourself. Really, when it comes to what to do on the date, you're limited only by your creativity.

Museums, a picnic in the park, or a hike are also great cheap or free options. (If you're doing something like going for a hike, bike ride, or similar outdoor activity, make sure you choose a well-traveled path and that someone else knows where you're going to be. Safety first!)

Q: Is it true that GLBTQ people are more promiscuous? Should I expect physical contact on the date?
A: Myth alert! That's not true. Queer people are, by nature, no more promiscuous than their straight counterparts. And you certainly shouldn't feel like you have to engage in sexual activity to find out if you're GLBTQ, to prove something to someone (even yourself), to make another person happy, or for any other reason. Just like anyone else, you should take the time you need to be sure you're absolutely, positively ready and that the other person is the one you're ready to share that part of yourself with.

Q: If I don't know a lot of GLBTQ people, will I just have to settle for dating whoever is around?
A: Absolutely not. One of the downsides of being GLBTQ in middle or high school is that you probably have fewer dating options than some of your straight friends. Nevertheless, you don't have to settle. If someone doesn't particularly interest you, you don't have to date him or her just because he or she is one of the only GLBTQ people you know.

What's My Type?

Among the most common misconceptions about GLBTQ people is that we always pair off according to type—butch with femme. Thankfully, with today's younger generation, these ideas are starting to change. Words like butch (people having a traditionally masculine gender expression) and femme (people having a traditionally feminine gender expression) don't even begin to take into account the full spectrum of GLBTQ people; many don't consider themselves to be one or the other. Also, attraction just is, whether you're GLBTQ or straight. Even if your taste leans one way or the other, who you end up with may very well surprise you.

The concepts of butch and femme have been around a long time. In the past, they were often used as a visible means of declaring an interest in the same sex. The roles of butch and femme continue to influence some GLBTQ relationships, and there's nothing wrong with that. But they definitely don't have to.

These stereotypes also color the perception many straight people have about GLBTQ relationships. Many of the ideas are based on the concept that there has to be a male and a female in every relationship, and regardless of the sex or gender of those involved, each must take one of these roles. The truth is, so many people have been operating with these traditions for so long that they started to think of them as laws of nature. But they're not.

Some people choose this kind of dynamic in their relationships. But you also have a choice—you can be in a relationship with anyone regardless of what labels you take for yourselves, even if you don't take any labels at all.

BEEN THERE

"The dynamics of queer relationships aren't talked about very often. Ideas of butch and femme within relationships are things that are stereotyped about the queer community, but rarely addressed in a plain way. At least in my experience of being bisexual, it can be really confusing to feel like there are specific male/female roles in a different-sex relationship and then not to have that framework, or familiarity, in same-sex relationships." —Gwen, 18

The GLBTQ Dating Scene: A Word of Caution

Meeting other queer teens can be difficult, but it also might not be as hard as you think. If you decide that it's time to date, be sure that you're safe in how and where you meet people. Some young people, distressed about being GLBTQ or just desperate to meet someone else who is, hook up with the first person who pays them attention.

Just like any dating situation, sometimes people don't have your best interests at heart. Although it's the exception rather than the rule, sometimes older and more experienced GLBTQ people take advantage of those who are younger or less experienced. These older individuals might offer teens sympathy and compassion while luring them into sexual situations. Sometimes they try to convince others that having sex will make them feel better or help them figure out who they are. It can be very comforting and flattering to have someone listen and pay attention to you— maybe he's the first queer person who's shown an interest in you. But take time to think about whether that person is thinking about you or about his own interests and agenda.

Being "Out" on a Date

It's great to hold hands with your sweetie or give her a little kiss while you're walking down the street. Unfortunately, public displays of affection (PDA) aren't something that queer people can always take for granted. It's important, especially as a young person, to be aware of where you are and who else is around.

It's one thing for your hand-holding to cause Grandma's jaw to drop in surprise. It's another for the action to attract the attention of people who might want to hurt you. That's not to say you can never give a smooch or put your arm around your guy in public. Just be smart about where you are and who is around. If PDA could cause a safety issue, you may want to give it a second thought. It's a lot better if the date is memorable because it went so well than because someone got hurt.

Assessing the Situation

Homophobes aren't lurking in every shadow, but they are out there—including some who are dangerous. Unless you're on extremely familiar or otherwise safe turf, like a GLBTQ establishment or event, before leaning in for a peck, do a quick check of your surroundings.

- Are a lot of people close by?
- What's the feeling you get from them by looking at them? What are your instincts telling you?
- Are people minding their own business, or do they seem a little too interested in yours?
- Are you in a place that's open or easily accessible, or are you in a confined space where it would be tough to leave quickly?

Keep in mind that the degree to which you're open about your identity will always be up to you. Be realistic about your safety. Hopefully, before too long, society will discover other things to worry about and a little queer PDA won't cause a second glance.

Knowing Looks and Open Stares

Even if you're not overtly displaying affection, people might know by looking at you and a date that you're out together. It might draw some attention. For example, maybe the woman at the table next to you nearly dropped her fork when you reached over and touched your date's hand. Assuming you're in a safe situation, it's up to you to decide whether you're comfortable with that.

Maybe you couldn't care less and say, "Let them stare until their eyes dry out." But if you're uncomfortable, this might be one of those times to remind yourself that there is absolutely, positively nothing wrong with being GLBTQ. It's natural to feel self-conscious when you start dating. In fact, queer or straight, young or old, most people feel self-conscious on first dates. Don't worry—it will get better. The longer you're out, the more comfortable with yourself you'll be.

And don't assume people are looking because they're upset or shocked. Maybe they think you make a cute couple, or perhaps the woman who almost dropped her fork became lost in thought wishing her daughter could find such a nice girl. You never know.

Singing the Breakup Blues

Sadly, not all love stories end happily. All romantic relationships can run into problems, and those between GLBTQ people are no different. Dealing with a breakup can be rough. Sometimes it can be tougher for queer teens because you might have limited options for people to talk with about the breakup.

If you're going through a breakup, it's important to do things to take care of yourself. Here are some tips for getting through what can be a difficult time.

1. Don't act like it didn't happen. Breakups hurt—that's why the word starts with "break." It's okay and natural to be upset.

2. Let it out. It's important not to bottle up your feelings. Write a top 10 list in your journal of why you're upset. Turn up your MP3 player and sing along at the top of your lungs to the most depressing or empowering songs you can find. Go for a run and tackle the toughest hill in the neighborhood. Express your feelings and release strong emotions in healthy ways.

3. Talk a good friend's ear off. Sharing your thoughts with another person can help you decompress. Don't forget your friends online, too. Reach out for some cyber support.

4. Take care of yourself. The worse you feel, the more important it is to show yourself some TLC. Try to eat well, stay hydrated, exercise, and get enough sleep. Maybe pamper yourself with a bubble bath and a good book or try yoga and meditation— whatever helps you relax and process the intense emotions you're experiencing.

5. Take it one day at a time. You won't be over a breakup in a day, or even two. But time does help, and you *will* start to feel better. You might even be ready to stop sticking pins into that little doll named after your ex. Seriously, though, breakups are part of life. They're hard, but they provide learning experiences and help shape who you are. Reflect on what you can learn from the experience.

In addition to the usual breakup complications, GLBTQ teens sometimes have another issue to face—people who know about the breakup might be pretty insensitive. Unfortunately, some people don't think queer relationships are as meaningful and valid as straight relationships. When you go through a breakup, they may not understand why you're so upset.

These people might say uninformed things, like encourage you to give being straight "another chance." Dealing with issues like that can be annoying and painful when you're trying to mend a broken heart.

Abusive Relationships: Recognizing Them and Getting Help

Dating violence can involve physical harm and sexual assault, such as nonconsensual sexual activity and rape. It can also include psychological or emotional abuse—including controlling behaviors or jealousy. Both female and male teens can be victims and/or perpetrators of dating violence. Although little research exists on dating violence among queer teens, research on same-gender violence among GLBTQ adults shows violence patterns similar to those among heterosexual adults.

More than 20 percent of adolescents say they've experienced emotional abuse or physical violence from an intimate partner. And this number is thought to be underreported, perhaps due to shame about being in an abusive relationship, concern about the abusive partner finding out, or fear of losing the relationship. Those in same-sex relationships sometimes are reluctant to report abuse because they aren't ready to come out about their sexual orientation. Some researchers estimate that it's closer to 30 percent of adolescents who have been harmed by partners.

Abuse between male partners may be overlooked because a conflict between men might be considered a fair fight. This is simply not true. Abuse of any kind is *never* acceptable. According to data from the National Coalition of Anti-Violence Programs, those who reported abuse in GLBTQ relationships are almost equally divided between male and female.

Dating violence for GLBTQ young people is very similar to abuse and violence in straight teen relationships, but queer teens may face additional challenges. They may have to deal with homophobia and ignorance about GLBTQ relationships. Abusive partners also might threaten to out the person being abused.

GLBTQ teens might struggle with ideas of what relationships should be like because relatively few positive queer role models are available. This can make abuse harder to recognize because victims don't expect it or see it addressed in GLBTQ relationships. No matter who you're dating, you have the right to be treated with respect by your partner. There is no excuse for abusive behavior of any kind, period.

BEEN THERE

"The healthiest relationships are based on mutual respect. They are partnerships that give you energy and bring intimacy into life without harming your other relationships." —Jeremy, 20

Here are some facts about dating violence and relationship abuse for GLBTQ teens:

- You never deserve to be abused. No one does.
- The abuse is not your fault. It's the fault of the abuser, no matter how much that person might blame you. ("You shouldn't have said that. You know I have a temper.")
- Abuse can take many different forms. It can be physical, emotional, sexual, psychological, verbal, or even social (like trying to turn friends against you or posting harassing comments about you on a website).
- Abuse usually happens in cycles. There might be a lot of kissing and making up afterwards, but eventually the abuse starts all over again.
- Abusers often try to isolate their partners from family, friends, and teammates. The person being abused often feels scared and alone.
- Abuse is about control and power, *not* love.

Dating violence and relationship abuse are serious problems for queer and straight teens alike. The good news is many more domestic violence resources are available today for GLBTQ people. If you're in an abusive relationship and need help getting out, many organizations can provide assistance.

Kinds of Dating Violence and Relationship Abuse

Many types of abuse happen in relationships. It's good to know what they are so you can recognize them right away if they occur.

Emotional Abuse. Emotional abuse can be harder to recognize than other forms of abuse, because it is often less obvious than physical abuse. Emotional abuse can include name-calling, insults, your partner putting you and your interests down, jealousy and possessiveness, and attempts to control who you see, what you do, what you wear, even what you eat.

A partner might tell you that you're fat or stupid or that no one else would ever want you. If you complain about this treatment, he might tell you it's not a big deal or you're too sensitive. Maybe your partner is extremely jealous and always demands to know where you are and who you're with. Or maybe he controls you with the fear of what he will do if he loses his temper (like breaking things, humiliating you in public, or hurting you). Perhaps he makes extreme demands on your time (even when you have important school or family commitments) and flirts, pouts, and eventually loses his temper if he doesn't get his way. Maybe he tells you in subtle or obvious ways that you could never find someone

Abusive Relationships: Getting Help

National Domestic Violence Hotline (1-800-799-7233). It can be difficult to break out of an abusive relationship. You might need help. If you're in an abusive relationship or concerned a friend or family member needs help, call or visit the website (www.thehotline.org) for free 24-7 support and referrals to local services.

The Rape, Abuse and Incest National Network (RAINN) (1-800-656-4673). RAINN offers extensive resources and assistance for sexual assault, including the hotline listed, or go to their website (www.rainn.org) for an online helpline. RAINN also can connect you with state or local domestic violence coalitions and rape or sexual violence crisis centers.

better than him. Whatever the method, it's all abuse. Emotional abuse can take a lot of different forms, but they all have the same result—they make you feel bad about yourself.

Physical Abuse. Physical abuse often is the first thing that comes to mind when people think about abusive relationships. Such abuse can include hitting, slapping, shoving, grabbing, kicking, hair pulling, biting, pinching, and throwing things. Physical abuse often is accompanied by threats of violence or an ongoing fear that violence will erupt if the abused partner does or says the wrong thing.

Sexual Abuse. Physical abuse can also be sexual in nature. Sexual abuse can include being forced or coerced into doing sexual activities you don't want to do or aren't ready for. The abusive partner might use emotional blackmail like, "If you really love me . . ." to pressure you into sexual activity.

It's important to remember that even if you have a sexual relationship with your partner, you always have the right to say no to physical or sexual contact of any kind. It doesn't matter how long you've been dating. It's your body. Even if you've been sexual with your partner before, you still have the right to say no now. If your partner doesn't respect that and tries to force or coerce you, that's abuse.

BEEN THERE

"I was in a relationship for a few years and I actually thought it was a good one. I mean, we loved each other — what else do you need? Periodically, though, she'd tell me stuff like that I was difficult or that other people didn't really like me that much. If I told her I was hurt by what she said, she'd tell me, 'You're just too sensitive.' She'd also imply that I was lucky she put up with me. I eventually broke up with her and it wasn't until I was out of the relationship for a while and had a new, healthy one that I realized just how unhealthy that other relationship was. I think because she never hit me and she was so fun a lot of the time I just overlooked the other stuff. But it took me a long time to repair the damage to my self-esteem that relationship had done." —Carmen, 19

An Abusive Relationship Self-Test

It can be hard to recognize abuse when you're close to someone. Here are some questions to help you take a closer look at your situation. If you answer "yes" to any of these questions, you could be in an abusive relationship:

- Does your partner call you names, insult you, or make you feel bad about yourself?
- Does your partner often demand to know where you've been (or are going) and who you talk to, call, email, or text?
- Does your partner try to control who you connect with online at social networking sites?
- Does your partner humiliate you, including in public or at school?
- Does your partner make all of the decisions in the relationship or get ugly when you disagree with what he wants?
- Do you make decisions about what you'll do or who you'll talk to based on how you think your partner will react?
- Does your partner try to control what you wear and/or what you eat? Does she make negative comments about your appearance?
- Are you ever afraid of your partner?
- Does your partner ever blame you for his behavior, telling you that it's your fault he hit you, scared you, or lost his temper?
- Do you find yourself making excuses to others for your partner's behavior, especially how she treats you?
- Does your partner try to keep you from spending time with your family or friends?
- Is your partner inconsiderate of your feelings? Does he tell you that you're blowing things out of proportion or that you're overreacting when you try to discuss his behavior?
- Is your partner jealous of your time? Does she insist on being with you constantly?
- Does your partner ever force or coerce you into engaging in intimate physical contact?
- Has your partner ever physically assaulted you, regardless of whether he caused a bruise or other injury?
- Has your partner ever verbally assaulted or threatened you?
- Has your partner ever destroyed any of your possessions or done something else to "punish" you?

- Has your partner ever threatened to hurt you or herself if you leave the relationship?

If one or more of these sounds familiar, you might be in an abusive relationship.

Stopping Abuse

Abuse is never acceptable. It is your right to leave an abusive (or any) relationship immediately. If you identify abuse (or patterns that could lead to it) in your relationship and want to address it with your partner, here is some guidance that could help.

1. *Tell him how his words or actions make you feel.* Emphasize that it's your right to feel safe and supported in relationships.
2. *If he is apologetic and seems genuinely remorseful, it's up to you whether you want to give him another chance.* But be very careful. Abusive relationships often have cycles. The abusive person is very apologetic for what he's done and swears he will "never do it again." Things are good for a while, but then the old pattern of abuse can start again.
3. *If the abuse starts again, it's time to get out.* Everyone makes mistakes, but chances are the abuse is part of a cycle, and it's only a matter of time before that behavior shows itself again.

▼ **What If It's You?** What if you're worried that *you* are the one treating your partner disrespectfully or abusively? Recognizing this is a very important step. Consider these questions: Is this the type of person you want to be? Is this the kind of relationship you want to have, instead of one built on mutual respect and trust? There can be a lot of reasons why you're treating your partner abusively. Maybe this is the kind of relationship your parents or other family members have. You might need to get support for emotional issues you're dealing with. It's not too late to get help. You, too, can call any of the resources listed in this chapter or talk to a trusted adult. Do it not just for your partner, but also for yourself. ▼

If you decide to get out of the relationship entirely, you have options. You can call national hotlines (like the ones listed on page 105) or identify local resources by looking in a phone directory or searching online. Domestic violence organizations, rape crisis centers, and GLBTQ resource centers are all good places to start.

It can be difficult to reach out to people you know, but trusted adults can also provide support. Adults at home, older siblings, GSA sponsors, or trusted school officials are all possibilities. If you're not out to anyone, talking with someone in your life might not be an option. You can talk to someone anonymously at a local or national organization.

You Deserve R-E-S-P-E-C-T

Soul singer Aretha Franklin had it right. Respect is the word to remember in relationships. Keep these tips in mind to be sure your relationships are healthy.

React to your partner's negative behavior by talking to her or getting out of the relationship.

Express your ideas and thoughts. If your partner tries to make you think or act a certain way, he's bad news.

Spend your time only with people who are supportive and positive. If this doesn't include your partner, leave her behind.

Pledge to yourself that you value your own well-being too much to tolerate an abusive relationship.

Expect to have a partner who respects you and who you respect in turn.

Choose for yourself. Don't let your partner dictate your decisions about who you talk to, what you eat, how you dress, or anything else.

Talk to someone if you are in an abusive relationship. Tell this person you need help putting a stop to the abuse. It's okay to ask for help.

Chapter 7

Sex and Sexuality

Love is a many gendered thing.

If you're thinking about relationships and dating, you're probably also thinking a bit (or maybe a lot) about your sexuality. Like relationships, sexuality can be a confusing and complicated issue. What works for one person might not for another. How do you know what you're ready for, or if you're even ready for a physical relationship? It can help to think about what questions you have and what you feel comfortable with *before* you end up in a position where you're confronted with decisions about physical intimacy.

Especially for GLBTQ teens, reliable information about sex can be tough to come by. You might feel that what you're hearing about sex from your friends, family members, adults at school, or religious leaders doesn't apply to you. If most everyone around you is assuming you're straight and has traditional ideas of sexuality and gender, getting the information you need about sex can seem impossible.

Making good decisions about sexual activity is tremendously important. When are you ready? What boundaries do you want to set for yourself with regard to physical intimacy? How well do you need to know or how much do you need to care for someone before you're ready to be intimate? What are you comfortable doing? What do you think sex is and what does it mean to you? Do you know how to stay safe sexually? Are you able to talk to someone you're dating about what your limits are for keeping yourself healthy physically and emotionally?

That's a lot to think about, and trying to process all of these questions can feel overwhelming. But they're important questions to answer *before* you start to engage in sexual activity. Don't feel discouraged. Accurate information is your best friend, and it is out there. What you know or learn about yourself, about what you believe, and about sex and sexuality will help guide you through your questions and help you make decisions that are right for you.

Beliefs—what you think is right and wrong and what you believe is important—are what people use to figure out their own behavior and their boundaries. People often develop their beliefs from their family, culture, and religion or spirituality. You might be comfortable with these beliefs based on this input, or you might choose to explore different beliefs. Adolescence is a very important time for establishing your independence and determining what beliefs you will adopt as your own.

If you can be open with family members, spiritual leaders, or others in your life, they might be able to help you think through your questions about what's right and wrong. They could help you think about what type of person you want to be. If you come from a religious, cultural, or family belief system that strongly disapproves of queer people, figuring out what you believe in can be more complicated. It can help to talk about your thoughts and feelings with a counselor or health/sexuality educator who is knowledgeable about GLBTQ issues. Or maybe there is another objective person you can trust who will listen without judgment and provide unbiased feedback.

The other information you need is the technical stuff about sex, sexuality, and how our bodies work. Questions like "What is queer sex?" and "What is safer sex?" are important to answer. This chapter is designed to help you recognize myths and misinformation about queer sex and sexuality and to give you some facts.

When information about sex is presented at school or at home, the usual assumption is that your partner will be someone of the opposite sex. Many parents don't think to raise the issue of GLBTQ sexuality when they're talking about sex. They might focus on discussing (or lecturing on) anatomy, pregnancy, abstinence, or sexually transmitted infections (STIs). Also, if your parents are straight, their understanding of queer physical relationships is likely to be limited or nonexistent. And some parents, regardless of whether their kids are GLBTQ or straight, never have "the talk," leaving you to get information about sex—accurate or inaccurate—from teachers or peers. Or you might not get any information at all.

When schools teach topics about human sexuality, they often avoid discussing queer relationships or gloss over the topic. A 2007 study of health education programs conducted by the Centers for Disease Control's (CDC) Division of Adolescent and School Health (DASH) found that 48 percent of U.S. schools taught about sexual identity and sexual orientation.

According to the "2009 National School Climate Survey" published by GLSEN, only 23 percent of students reported inclusion of GLBTQ-related topics in any of their classes. And only 4 percent of students said that GLBTQ-related information was included in their health classes.

The fact that most schools don't mention queer sexuality in their curricula might leave you feeling invisible and uninformed. For example, advice like, "Wait until you're married" isn't particularly useful to GLBTQ people who, at least for now, can't be legally married in most states.

You have a lot to think about before you decide what's right for you. This chapter will give you tools to make the choices that are healthiest for you based on your personal beliefs.

Making Sound Decisions About Sex

Becoming aware of your sexuality is a major part of adolescence, whether you're queer or straight. It can involve a lot of thinking about sex and what it means for you. It also involves making a lot of decisions.

Deciding to be sexually active is a big choice and a major milestone for many reasons. It can involve new physical experiences, intense emotions, and new responsibilities. Depending on the situation, you might find yourself needing to know a lot of things at once—from understanding how to keep yourself safe and healthy to being able to communicate honestly with a partner. Taking the time now to determine boundaries and get accurate information is an important way to respect and care for yourself.

You might decide not to have sex right now, to experiment with some activities but draw the line at others, or to actually have sex. In some ways you might feel ready, but in other ways you might not. You might have a lot of curiosity and a mix of facts and misinformation buzzing around in your mind. And that can lead to a lot of questions. Here are some common ones:

Q: I have sexual urges. Does that mean I'm ready?
A: As you become more sexually aware, you're also changing emotionally. You could be having physical urges—which is completely normal—but you might also feel confused, worried, anxious, or unsure about acting on those urges.

There isn't a magic age when someone becomes ready to have sex. The factors that contribute to being emotionally and physically ready are personal and unique to each individual.

Q: Can I be sort of ready?
A: If you feel like you're ready for sexual intimacy or sexual activity, that doesn't necessarily mean you're ready for sex. Thankfully, it doesn't have to be all or nothing. From holding hands and hugging to making out and beyond, many activities can be healthy expressions of affection and be both physically and emotionally pleasurable. You could be ready for some of them, but not yet others. *If you're doing something that makes you feel uncomfortable, listen to that feeling.* It might be an indicator that you're moving beyond what you're ready for.

It's up to you to set your boundaries. Learning how to set those boundaries is part of the process of maturing into someone who's comfortable being affectionate or sexual with someone else. Part of setting boundaries is being able to communicate with your partners even when the topic is embarrassing or difficult. Think about what you want and what's important to you. Talk with your partner about your feelings, and ask what your partner feels ready for. You might be ready for different things.

Gradually exploring is usually safer and more comfortable than jumping right in and "going all the way." It also allows you to move at your own pace and decide one step at a time what you're ready for and what's too much, for now.

Q: Isn't pretty much everyone having sex?
A: It's true that there are many teens who engage in sexual activity. There are also many teens who choose to wait or who set boundaries about their sexual activities. Doing it and feeling like you made the right decision can be two different things. Consider some research results:

The Sexuality Information and Education Council of the United States (SIECUS) surveyed American adults about the first time they had sex and found that more than 80 percent were teens when they first had sex. *However*, many of those people, when looking back, weren't happy with their decisions. SIECUS reported that 65 percent of women and 45 percent of men regretted their decisions and thought they had sex at too early an age.

According to the CDC's "Youth Risk Behavior Surveillance, 2009," 46 percent of high school students had engaged in sexual intercourse. So although it might seem like it, not everyone is having sex. If you decide you're not ready or you're not interested, you'll have a lot of company (54 percent of your peers, to be precise).

Researchers have also found that some teens who tell their peers they've had sex are stretching the truth. With all the pressure to have sex, it's understandable that some teens feel the need to lie about their experiences. Some tell stories to get attention, to feel more mature, or to get people to quit asking if they're having sex. Knowing that they could be lying gives you another reason not to base your decisions on what your friends might or might not be doing.

If your friends really are having sex, you might feel left out or like they're growing up and you're not. Keep reminding yourself that what might be right for them isn't necessarily right for you. Only you can decide what you're ready for. Besides, if your friends are worth keeping, they won't pressure you to do anything that's not right for you.

When the Pressure's On It can be hard to say no to sex when someone is pressuring you. You might have to let them know that you want the pressure to stop. Here are some possible responses:

Pressure	Response
"You should really try it. It's great."	"I'm sure it *will* be great . . . when I'm ready. I don't want to do something I think I'll regret. And if you really care about me, you won't put pressure on me."
"Don't be such a prude. Everyone's doing it."	"Not really. A lot of people might say they're doing it, but not all of them are telling the truth. I'm my own person. I'm not concerned about what other people are doing."
"Sex is no big deal."	"If that were true, we wouldn't be having this conversation. If sex is no big deal, why do you care so much about whether I'm having it? The way I look at it, what I do with my body *is* a big deal."
"Maybe you're just not mature enough to have sex."	"I'm mature enough to make responsible decisions about things that are important to me and that will affect my life. I'm mature enough to stick to those decisions. And I'm also mature enough not to pressure my friends into doing something they've decided isn't right for them."

Q: Sex is only right when you're in love, right?
A: For some, sex is an expression of love between two people. For others, it's a physical pleasure that doesn't have to be accompanied by love. Even so, most people agree that the most fulfilling sexual experiences are those that happen with someone you care about. Still, being in love doesn't mean you have to have sex.

Ways to Say No to a Boyfriend or Girlfriend
Saying no to a partner who wants to be sexual can be extremely difficult. But you don't owe it to anyone to have sex. Your first responsibility is to yourself. The only one who's looking out for you is you, so you owe it to yourself to make the decision that's best for you.

Here are some tips for responding to pressure from a boyfriend or girlfriend:

Pressure	Response
"If you love me, you'll have sex with me."	"Sex and love are two different things. If *you* love *me,* you'll let me choose when I'm ready. Besides, if you push me into making a decision I'm not comfortable with, it could ruin our relationship. Is having sex worth that risk to you?"
"You say you love me, so prove it."	"I prove to you that I love you every day by respecting your thoughts and decisions. Why don't you prove *you* love *me* by doing the same?"
"It's not like you can get pregnant."	"Maybe not, but having sex means a lot to me. If I decide to have sex with you, then I'm deciding to share something very personal and intimate. Acting like sex is no big deal tells me that you don't respect how important the decision is for me. I'm not comfortable with that."
"It's not like you're going to get married. So what are you saving yourself for?"	"I'm saving myself for when I'm ready and when I've found the right person. If you can't respect my decisions, you're not that person."
"C'mon. I know you're not a virgin."	"Just because I've had sex before doesn't mean I want to have it now. And it doesn't mean that I'll do it with just anyone. I respect myself, and I give serious thought to who I'm intimate with."
"But we've had sex before."	"I know, but the way I felt afterward made me know I wasn't ready. So now I'm going to wait until I am. If you can't support my decision, you're sending me a message that sex means more to you than my feelings and our relationship."

BEEN THERE

"Don't let sex be the reason you are with the person you're with. Being sexually active is nothing compared with the emotional and mental connection that is important in the relationship." — Raina, 20

Q: But I'm in a relationship . . .
A: Love and sex are not synonymous. You can love someone, yet not feel ready to have sex. It doesn't mean you don't care about that person. It means you don't want or aren't ready to move to that level of physical intimacy just yet.

One of the absolute best things about being in a relationship is the firsts—the first time your eyes meet and you smile at each other, the first time you hold hands, the first time you kiss, and if everything feels right, the first time you have sex. But the thing that makes those firsts so special and memorable is that they happen only once, and they're most enjoyable when you're both ready.

Q: What if I don't want to keep having sex?
A: Maybe you've already started having sex. If you're having sex and you're not feeling good about it, remember that *you can stop*. Just because you've had it doesn't mean you have to keep having it.

Have an open discussion with your partner. If he really cares about you, he'll understand and will be supportive. Bringing it up might feel a little scary or embarrassing, but if you don't feel like you can talk to your partner about sex, it could be a signal that you've gotten into something too soon or with the wrong person.

BEEN THERE

"I've never been sexually active. I plan to wait." — Julio, 19

What Do You Think?

You might have a lot on your mind right now regarding your sexuality and having sex. Maybe the questions and situations you've been reading about are familiar, or perhaps you're asking yourself other questions. Perhaps you're just starting to think about these issues, or you may already be sexually active. Either way, the more you know about yourself, the healthier your decisions will be about your boundaries, activities, and partners.

Here are some helpful questions to ask yourself and think about while you're deciding if you're ready to be (or to continue being) sexually active:

- Am I comfortable with myself and my body?
- Do I respect myself and have a strong sense of my own self-worth?
- Am I comfortable talking about sex and my boundaries with my partner?
- Do I feel comfortable saying no when I need to?
- Have I thought about what being sexual could mean for me emotionally and what it could mean for my relationship?
- Do I understand that I don't need to have sex to be loved? Do I understand that just because I love someone, I don't need to have sex to prove it?
- Do I know what STIs are and how they're transmitted? Do I know about safer sex? Am I able to talk to my partner about safer sex? Am I confident enough to insist on using protection for any sexual activity?
- Do I know that I can change my mind at any time about having sex? Do I understand that I can say no at any point, even at the last minute, even if I've told someone that I will have sex, and even if I've said yes before?
- Do I know that if I have sex, I don't have to keep having it?
- Do I feel clear about my beliefs and values about having sex?

Five Myths (and Truths) About GLBTQ Sex

Arm yourself with the facts before you make any decisions about sex. Thinking about sex and sexuality can make teens nervous and confused. This can be especially true for young people who are GLBTQ, in part because there is so much misinformation about queer sex and sexuality. Don't let your decisions about sex be influenced by myths and stereotypes.

Here are some of the more common myths about GLBTQ sexuality:

Myth #1: Having sex is the best way to help me figure out if I'm GLBTQ. Many people are faced with questions like "How do I know for sure?" when they're coming out. Some people might even tell you that if you've never had sex with someone of the same sex, you can't be certain of your sexual orientation. Many people believe that being GLBTQ is about who you have sex with.

Truth #1: It's not. Being queer is about who you are as a person, and it's part of your identity. It's also about who you are *emotionally* attracted to. Having sex won't prove or disprove anything that you didn't already know or suspect. So being sexually active is not the answer. And having sex could have negative results if you're not ready to deal with the emotions it can stir up or aren't comfortable insisting on safer sex.

Myth #2: GLBTQ people are promiscuous. Some people have the idea that being GLBTQ is only about sex, and therefore having sex is the primary focus of queer people.

Truth #2: The fact is, GLBTQ people aren't any more promiscuous by nature or in practice than straight people. Being GLBTQ doesn't mean you have to engage in sexual activity. Having sex is a personal decision, regardless of whether you're queer or straight.

Myth #3: Oral sex doesn't count as sex. Some people consider oral sex to be a very intimate sexual activity, while others attach less importance to it. Some people feel it's an activity you do as part of getting ready to have sex. Others consider it to be sex— for them, it's a primary sexual activity.

Truth #3: Here are some truths to consider about oral sex. There's no denying that oral sex is significant sexual contact. You definitely can get or give many sexually transmitted infections (STIs) through oral sex. Oral sex involves very intimate physical contact, and you're making a choice to share something very personal with someone else. As a matter of self-respect, you'll want to spend some time considering who, if anyone right now, is worthy of that level of intimacy with you.

It's important to communicate clearly about this issue with your partner. If oral sex is a big deal for you, but your partner doesn't feel the same, it can cause a problem. You could end up feeling like your partner doesn't appreciate the value of physical intimacy and how important sharing that is to you. Determining whether you're ready to engage in sexual activity includes making important decisions about oral sex.

Myth #4: Gay men only engage in anal sex and lesbians only engage in oral sex. This is one of the most pervasive sexual myths about GLBTQ people. The myth comes from people who don't know or understand what it means to be queer, so their ideas about queer sexuality are limited and sometimes downright strange.

Truth #4: There is a whole range of sexual activities that GLBTQ people engage in. Some gay men rarely or never have anal sex and some lesbians rarely or never have oral sex. It's up to each individual to decide what he or she likes and is comfortable with.

BEEN THERE

"Sex is not the end-all, be-all. Having sex does not make or break one's identity. Enjoy what you do because you want to be doing it, not because you think it's what you should be doing."
— Joseph, 20

Myth #5: Only people who are GLBTQ get HIV/AIDS. In the early 1980s, when the HIV and AIDS epidemic was first starting in the United States, gay men were severely impacted. Many people grew to associate gay men and queer people in general with AIDS, even though all different kinds of people were becoming sick.

Truth #5: *Everyone* has to worry about HIV/AIDS, GLBTQ or straight. Contrary to what some people believe, gay men are not solely responsible for the spread of HIV/AIDS. It is a worldwide pandemic that affects people of all ages, races, genders, and orientations. According the Joint United Nations Programme on HIV/AIDS (UNAIDS) and the World Health Organization (WHO), more than 33 million people worldwide are living with HIV or AIDS. Forty percent of new HIV infections worldwide occur among heterosexual young people. That's more than any other group, including homosexuals.

It's not who you are, but what you do that puts you at risk for contracting HIV/AIDS. And you can get HIV/AIDS from only one exposure. It's not the number of times you have sex, but rather the kind of sex you have that puts you at risk. If you make healthy choices and practice safer sex (more on that later), you can decrease your risk of HIV exposure, but there is no such thing as 100 percent safe sex for anyone—GLBTQ or straight.

The Big Picture: STIs and Pregnancy

Some other issues to consider when making decisions about intimate relationships are sexually transmitted infections (STIs) and pregnancy. Yes, pregnancy. Being queer might make it less likely, but it doesn't make it impossible. (For more about this, see page 122.) And if you are thinking about becoming (or already are) sexually active, you definitely need to think about STIs, whether you're GLBTQ or straight. STIs are infections passed from one person to another primarily through vaginal, oral, or anal intercourse, although intimate contact without intercourse can also transmit several STIs. STIs are serious business. Unfortunately, one encounter (with or without protection) can result in some serious and long-term consequences.

Just the Facts About STIs

1. STIs are common among teens. The Centers for Disease Control (CDC) reports that each year, more than 19 million new STI cases occur. Nearly half of these occur in people ages 15 to 24. According to the American Social Health Association (ASHA), half of all sexually active young people will contract an STI by age 25. The CDC states that in 2006, about 1 million adolescents and young adults ages 10 to 24 were reported to have chlamydia, gonorrhea, or syphilis. Syphilis cases among ages 15 to 24 have increased in both males and females in recent years.

It's important to understand, too, that people with STIs don't always have obvious symptoms. It's not uncommon for someone to have (and be transmitting) an STI without realizing it.

BEEN THERE
"I have always practiced safer sex because it is so essential for my health. It's important to know where to go for condoms and testing." —Priscilla, 20

2. HIV/AIDS still has no cure. There are many other STIs besides HIV/AIDS, but HIV infection among teens is a serious issue. ASHA reports that half of all new HIV infections occur among adolescents. The CDC states that in 2006, the majority of new diagnoses of HIV infection in the United States occurred among adolescent and young adult males ages 20 to 24.

While it's true many infected people are enjoying a better quality of life than ever before due to advances in drug therapies, living with HIV/AIDS is *not* easy. Even if researchers are successful developing a cure for HIV/AIDS and a vaccine to prevent it, it will likely be many years before either is available. In the meantime, HIV/AIDS transmission is a very real risk. New therapies for HIV/AIDS may give some people a misplaced feeling of security—they think they don't have to practice safer sex. It's tempting to give in to the moment, but that's a very risky gamble.

3. Women who have sex with women transmit STIs, too. Herpes, HPV (genital wart virus), and bacterial vaginosis are transmitted fairly easily between women during sex. Even though STIs like HIV, hepatitis B, gonorrhea, and chlamydia are less likely to be transmitted, it is still possible.

Pregnancy

Some teens, terrified by the idea they might be queer, have sexual relationships with people of the opposite sex to prove to themselves and others that they're straight. Others engage in heterosexual sex to find a social group they think of as being more "normal" than the queer community. They might believe that it would be "easier" to be straight.

Make no mistake, if you're an anatomical female who has vaginal intercourse with an anatomical male, you can get pregnant. Having a different sexual orientation or gender identity won't prevent a pregnancy. And if you're an anatomical male, even if you are gay or trans, you can get an anatomical female pregnant.

▼ More Information About Sex, STIs, and Being Safe

Scarleteen (www.scarleteen.com). Scarleteen provides positive, accurate, nonjudgmental information for young people about sex, including articles, advice, and interactive media. The site was founded by Heather Corinna, author of *S.E.X.: The All-You-Need-to-Know Progressive Sexuality Guide to Get You Through High School and College* (see Resources on page 207).

Sex, Etc. (www.sexetc.org). Sex, Etc., is part of the Teen-to-Teen Sexuality Education Project, a national initiative promoting comprehensive sexuality education for young people. The site provides extensive information on sexuality and sexual health, forums for teens to share their experiences, online chats with health experts, an extensive glossary of sex-related terms, and more.

Go Ask Alice! (www.goaskalice.com). Go Ask Alice! is a health Q&A website operated by the Alice! Health Program at Columbia University. The site includes factual information about sexuality, sexual health, and relationships. Post your own questions, read posts from others, and get answers from the experts.

I Wanna Know (www.iwannaknow.org). Sponsored by the American Social Health Association, this site provides teens with accurate, nonjudgmental information about STIs and sexual health. It includes information about specific STIs, how to prevent them, protection (including contraception), and how to get tested.

Lesbian, Gay, Bisexual, and Transgender Health (www.cdc.gov/lgbthealth). Operated by the Centers for Disease Control, this site has extensive information on sexuality and health issues for GLBTQ people.

Advocates for Youth (www.advocatesforyouth.org). Advocates for Youth has a Youth Activist Network that empowers teens to make healthy decisions about sexual activity. Visit the website for information about sexuality or to get involved in advocacy efforts.

CDC National STD Hotline (1-800-232-4636). A service of the CDC's National Center for HIV, STD, and TB Prevention, the National STD Hotline provides anonymous, confidential information on STIs and how to prevent them. It also provides referrals to clinical and other services. It operates 24 hours a day, seven days a week. ▼

Safe Sex vs. Safer Sex

What's the difference? The first is a myth—there is no such thing as totally safe sex. However, if you choose to be sexually active, practicing safer sex can significantly help reduce the chances of pregnancy or transmitting an STI.

Here are some basic facts you need to know about safer sex:

Fact: Bodily fluids such as semen, vaginal fluids, and blood are the primary means through which STIs pass from one person to another. It's not always necessary to exchange bodily fluids to become infected, but they are a primary means of infection for many STIs (and the only means through which HIV can be transmitted).

Fact: Latex barriers provide the most effective protection against infection. Whether it's in the form of condoms, dental dams, or gloves, latex is your best friend when it comes to safer sex. You can buy latex barriers at most pharmacies, convenience stores, and discount retailers. Some restrooms are even equipped with condom dispensers. Also, many public health clinics (including Planned Parenthood) and HIV/AIDS organizations give out free condoms. Some also give out dental dams.

A few other useful things to know about latex:

- Latex condoms are the best choice for safer sex. Some "natural" condoms are made from lambskin, which infections like HIV can pass through. Latex, when used properly, stops infections. If you're allergic to latex, see page 126 for information on polyurethane barriers.

- Dental dams are square pieces of latex designed to cover the vulva, vagina, or anus during oral sex. Dental dams protect the mouth from exposure to bodily fluids that could contain bacteria or viruses.
- Dental dams can be harder to find than condoms. One alternative is to fashion a dental dam out of a condom by unrolling it, cutting off the closed end, and cutting it along the long end. This only works with an unlubricated condom and also one that is not treated with a spermicide. Plastic wrap can also be used as a substitute for a dental dam, but it must be the kind that isn't perforated—plastic wrap with tiny holes in it is useless when it comes to preventing STI transmission.

Fact: Latex is essential not only for vaginal or anal sex, but also for oral sex and mutual masturbation. Infections can be passed during activities that include touching if a partner's hands or fingers have cuts, scratches, or other open abrasions or sores. You might not always see tiny abrasions, so it's best to use a latex glove or finger cots—latex coverings for individual fingers. These forms of protection can be found at most drugstores near first aid products or insulin test kits.

"Price Check on Condoms!" Nervous about going to the drugstore to buy protection? Part of gauging whether you're ready to engage in sexual behavior is assessing whether you're mature enough to practice safer sex. Keep in mind that it's better to have to visit the pharmacy for protection than it is to have to fill a prescription to treat an STI. If you're really nervous, think about asking a friend to go with you.

Fact: You must be careful with latex. It only works as long as it's undamaged. Heat and oil-based lubricants can damage latex. Don't keep latex barriers such as condoms in a wallet or somewhere else where they'll be exposed to prolonged heat. Also, don't use condoms or other latex barriers with oily substances such as baby oil, petroleum jelly, solid shortening, cooking oils (olive and vegetable oil), animal fats (including butter), massage oils, or peanut butter. Oils and petroleum-based products destroy latex.

The best bet for a lubricant is one that's water-based such as K-Y Jelly or K-Y Liquid, which you can find in most pharmacies and grocery stores. Some GLBTQ bookstores sell lubricants, as well. Silicone-based ones will also work. The packaging should indicate whether the lubricant is oil-, silicone-, or water-based.

Fact: Polyurethane and polyisoprene barriers can prevent transmission of HIV. Polyurethane and polyisoprene condoms, gloves, and dental dams—when properly used—do protect against HIV infection and the transmission of other STIs. The condoms also can be used to prevent pregnancy. However, according to the FDA and *Consumer Reports,* the condoms may be more prone to breaking. These options are usually recommended for people who are sensitive to latex or have a latex allergy.

Fact: Anal sex is a high-risk behavior and needs extra protection. It's one of the highest-risk behaviors for transmitting STIs, whether between partners of the same or opposite sex. The inside of the rectum is a very porous membrane that can transmit infection, including HIV contained in blood or semen, directly into the bloodstream. Unprotected anal sex has recently become popular among some people who have the misconception that HIV is no longer a concern. This is a myth. Anal sex is an *extremely* high-risk behavior for the transmission of HIV and other STIs.

Barriers to Safer Sex: Lack of Communication

Bring up safer sex with your partner while you're both fully clothed. Talking about issues that might make you shy or nervous is much easier when you're not in the heat of the moment.

Thinking and talking about safer sex ahead of time means you're giving yourself the opportunity to be prepared when the time comes. Make a point of knowing where you both stand so that you can respect each other's health and comfort levels. The keys to safer sex are openness and mutual respect.

BEEN THERE

"I had never been intimate with anyone before I was with my most recent girlfriend. But before we started to get sexually active, I had her show me her recent test results for STIs." —Vanessa, 19

Arguments Against Safer Sex and How You Can Handle Them

Here are some common arguments against safer sex and the opposite point of view:

Argument	The Other Side
"I'm allergic to latex."	It's true that some people are allergic to latex. However, due to wonderful scientific advances, condoms, dental dams, and gloves are available in polyurethane and polyisoprene, as well. A latex allergy is no excuse for not practicing safer sex. (For more about latex allergies, see page 126.)
"Safer is too complicated. It's better to just go with the flow."	If safer sex seems like a pain, how complicated is getting an infection or pregnant because you didn't feel like taking the time to use protection?
"It doesn't feel as good with a condom, dental dam, or glove."	What doesn't feel good is when partners don't consider each other's health and well-being. Show you care about yourself and your partner by practicing safer sex.
"It's embarrassing to talk with a partner about using protection."	Talking about safer sex can be uncomfortable. But look at it this way—if you're going to be sexually intimate with someone you should at least feel comfortable and respectful enough to get past a little embarrassment. Take a deep breath and insist that you both use protection.
"My partner says he's free of STIs, and I trust him."	It's great that you trust your partner, but that doesn't make you safe. Your partner might truly believe he's free of infection, just as you might believe the same about yourself. But many STIs don't have obvious symptoms, so it's important to be tested, then tested again a few months later. Out of concern and respect for yourself and your partner, play it safer.
"My partner and I are both virgins, so we don't need protection."	Even if you're both virgins (and people's definitions of virgin can vary), practices like anal sex can be risky because of the chance of infection due to possible exposure to bacteria. Also, if you're engaging in heterosexual sex, you can get pregnant even if it's your first time. Make sure your sexual experiences are healthy, both emotionally and physically.
"Talking about safer sex spoils the mood."	Talking about safer sex shows your partner that you care about both of you. And nothing spoils the mood like dealing with an STI. So talk to your partner about safer sex *before* you do anything, while your clothes are still on.

Think about how you want to keep yourself safe. It's not always easy to talk about safer sex, but you'll need to communicate with your partner about it. Even if you're not ready for sex, talk now so that when you *are* ready, you'll both be on the same page about practicing safer sex.

Barriers to Safer Sex: Drinking and Drugs

One of the biggest barriers to keeping yourself safe is drinking or doing drugs. Even with the best intentions, you can find yourself in the middle of activities or situations you would have avoided if you had been sober.

According to the National Institute on Drug Abuse:

- More than one-third of sexually active teens and young adults ages 15 to 24 report that alcohol or drug use has influenced a decision to do something sexual.
- Nearly a quarter of sexually active teens and young adults ages 15 to 24 report having unprotected sex because of alcohol or drug use.
- 43 percent of teens and young adults say they are concerned that they might do more sexually than they had planned because they are drinking or using drugs.

If your judgment is impaired, chances are greater that you'll have unsafe sex.

Drugs + sex = risky behavior. The best decisions are ones that you make when you're 100 percent sober.

Take time to explore your sexuality and sexual identity before expressing yourself physically with another person. If you're already engaging in sexual activity, check in with yourself. Figure out whether these activities are causing you stress or are bringing something positive to your life and your relationship. Sexual activity can be extremely positive and fulfilling if you approach it in a healthy way. That starts with self-awareness and a willingness to do what's best for you and potential partners.

Chapter 8
Staying Healthy

Queer by nature. Absolutely fabulous by choice.

For queer and questioning teens, adolescence can be an amazing and thought-provoking time. It can also come with its fair share of stress. In addition to normal adolescent changes, you might also be figuring out if you're GLBTQ, choosing whether or not to come out, and deciding how you feel about relationships and sex. With so much on your mind, it can be easy to lose track of taking care of yourself. But your physical and mental health are important and need attention just like other parts of your life.

Researchers from the American Psychological Association have noted that GLBTQ teens run a greater risk of taking part in potentially unhealthy or dangerous behaviors because of difficulty navigating the teen years. But they also noted that GLBTQ teens often have sophisticated ways of handling pressures and that they tend to use a broader range of coping resources than their heterosexual peers. GLBTQ teens may also be more likely to develop greater interpersonal problem-solving skills.

These latter findings are good news, because as a GLBTQ teen, you might face more difficult or complex challenges than your straight peers. This makes it even more important to pay attention to your health so you have the emotional and physical resources to deal with whatever life throws at you.

Chilling Out:
Dealing with Stress as a GLBTQ Teen

Anger, frustration, sadness—it's natural for young people to experience these feelings. According to the CDC's "Youth Risk Behavior Surveillance, 2009," 27 percent of 11th graders and 24 percent of 12th graders reported having prolonged feelings of sadness or hopelessness that prevented them from doing some of their usual activities. Nationwide, nearly 14 percent of students in grades 9–12 reported having seriously considered attempting suicide within the previous year.

These are alarming statistics, but it's believed the numbers are higher among GLBTQ students, because they're often dealing with issues related to sexual orientation and gender identity, as well as societal and peer pressures. This makes it especially important for you to have a game plan for how to cope during those times you may not be feeling your best.

BEEN THERE
"When I'm feeling down I sing or write. I try to do something creative; anything that will get my mind off of whatever is going on at that particular moment." —Eric, 15

Five Great Ways to Beat the Blues

It's okay to sometimes feel frustrated or unhappy with the way things are. But letting others' ignorant attitudes affect your mood over the long term won't make life better or easier. Help yourself feel better by finding positive ways to deal with difficult emotions. After all, you don't want to miss out on the wonderful things because you're stressed or depressed.

There are a lot of great, healthy ways to deal with stress on an everyday basis. Here are five basic things you can try.

1. Let it out! Find a way to express your feelings through talking, writing, dancing, acting, singing, rapping, or drawing. There's a whole range of great ways you can let it out. You can do this privately (write in a journal—see page 133—or dance in your room) or publicly (act in a school play or perform at an open mic night). The more ways you release stress, the better you can feel. You might even discover a talent you never knew you had.

2. Exercise. When you exercise, your brain releases chemicals called *endorphins* that help increase positive feelings and decrease feelings of pain or stress. Exercise is anything that gets you moving, including walking, shooting hoops, or playing a fitness video game.

▼ The Science of Stress

Stress isn't all bad. Technically, stress is the body's response to change. Some stress—like landing the lead in a musical—is positive stress (or *eustress*). Negative stress (or *distress*) results from difficult situations, like when a parent is sick or you're harassed at school. Eustress can make you feel hopeful, positive, and energized. Distress can leave you feeling anxious, sad, or out of control. When it's prolonged, it can have serious negative effects on your body.

Stress influences automatic responses in your nervous system called the parasympathetic (relaxation) response and the sympathetic (fight or flight) response. When you are relaxed, your body heals and restores itself, you're able to digest and absorb nutrition, and your muscles and heart rate relax—that's the parasympathetic response. Distress, however, triggers the opposite response—your body releases adrenaline, your heart rate increases, and internal healing processes nearly halt. If a close call, like a narrowly avoided car accident, has ever left you with your heart in your throat and hands shaking, you've experienced the sympathetic fight or flight response.

While some distress is normal, prolonged periods of it can result in serious physical problems. In the sympathetic state, your body starts to release a steroid hormone called cortisol. Too much cortisol has negative effects on your body, including decreased immune function, bone density, muscle tissue, and even brain function. It can also cause an increase in storage of abdominal fat. ▼

Exercise of all kinds can help you relieve stress—it's a matter of finding physical activities you enjoy doing. Try out for a team at school or join an intramural team in the community. (Some communities have GLBTQ sports teams, although they might be restricted to older teens or adults.) Or plan a game of your own. Get friends together to play volleyball, flag football, or whatever sport you enjoy. Classes in dance, yoga, or martial arts might all be options as well. If you prefer to go solo, try biking, skateboarding, inline skating, running, hiking, weight training, dancing, swimming, or doing parkour (free running, which includes jumping, flipping, and other acrobatic moves). Any kind of exercise can help you feel better emotionally and physically. So get those endorphins pumping and do something good for your body.

3. Eat well. A balanced diet with a lot of nutrients keeps your body healthy and happy. Eating only junk can increase feelings of tiredness and sadness. Especially now, when your body is maturing, it's important to eat a diet that's balanced among proteins, fats, and carbohydrates.

That doesn't mean you have to give up your favorite treats, but the key is to eat those things in moderation. You can have French fries or chocolate cake now and then, just don't make them staples of your diet. Good food gives your body and mind fuel to be strong and resilient. Drink plenty of water, too, to flush toxins from your body and keep your systems running their best.

4. Take healthy risks. Jump into life. One of the best things about being alive is trying new things. Sometimes those new things are scary, like trying out for that jazz band solo or asking someone out on a date. Sometimes they're fun, like joining a sports team, traveling somewhere you've never been, or discovering you're a master gardener. When you try new things, you can broaden your horizons while learning about yourself in the process. These experiences help focus your attention on positive things, rather than dwelling on life's challenges.

5. Get involved. Get involved in the GLBTQ community, whether it's by participating in an online forum or meeting other queer teens in real life. (Chapter 5, beginning on page 85, has information on how to do that.) Being involved can help you realize you're not alone and you don't have to feel isolated. It can be comforting to know there are a whole lot of us around from all walks of life. Volunteering for your favorite cause or getting politically active are also great ways to meet people—both queer and straight—who share your interests.

Jump Into Journaling

Keeping a journal is a great way to reflect on your life, work through feelings, and blow off steam. There are many different ways to keep a journal. You can write letters to people about how you feel (which you might or might not actually mail), sketch, write poetry, or just describe your day or feelings. Whatever form your journal takes, it's probably best to keep it hidden so you can feel free to really express yourself. If your journal is on a computer, password-protecting the document is a good idea.

Whether you're already a pro at journaling or just getting started, here is a strategy for writing when you feel stressed. It helps you let go of intense feelings and feel better about yourself at the same time.

1. In your journal (whether it's a notebook or on your computer) write down exactly what is making you stressed. Tell the person who made that nasty comment just what you think of it. Tell that senator you can't believe he sponsored that anti-queer bill. Whatever you're feeling, let it out.

2. Count the number of negative statements you made, like, "I can't believe he . . ." or "I am so sick of . . ."

3. Use a clean sheet of paper in your notebook or start a new page in your document. Make a numbered list for the negative statements. For example, if you wrote three negative things, number the list from one to three. Next to each number, write something positive about yourself. It doesn't have to have anything to do with being GLBTQ or even with what's upsetting you. This can be a good way to put things in perspective and get some emotional balance.

Here's an example of what this journal entry might look like:

I am sick of having to deal with the ignorance of some of my so-called peers.[1] Today, Isaiah made this really nasty comment about gay guys. And it was really loud, too. But Mrs. Jimenez didn't do anything about it. I can't stand her.[2] I told Alison about it during lunch and she agrees that Isaiah is a total jerk.[3]

1. I'm a good friend.
2. I'm sensitive to others' feelings.
3. I'm a great singer.

No matter how you choose to write in your journal, just remember three key words: *Let it out!* Bottling up feelings can build up stress and anxiety, which can take a mental and physical toll. It's important to let out feelings so you can move past them.

When Stress Turns Into Depression

Most young people have feelings of sadness or hopelessness from time to time, but queer teens often experience them more frequently than their heterosexual peers. Nothing about being GLBTQ means you're destined to be unhappy, but take the usual stresses of being a teen and combine them with confronting homophobia or transphobia (in peers or yourself), and you have a mixture that can take a toll on your self-esteem. Even if you're not facing harassment, you might not always feel like you fit in with the world around you. This can be true even if you generally feel good about yourself.

Studies, including the "Health and Risk Behaviors of Massachusetts Youth" report, consistently show that GLBTQ teens are up to four times more likely to attempt suicide than their heterosexual peers. The American Academy of Pediatrics cites a survey in which 28 percent of gay and bisexual teen-age boys and 20 percent of gay and bisexual teenage girls had attempted suicide. These statistics reveal the strong need for GLBTQ teens to be aware of the warning signs for depression (see page 137) and to get help if they need it.

BEEN THERE

"So many innocent teenagers end their own lives because of the ignorance out in the world. I mean, if high school is like this, what is the rest of the world like?" —Amar, 15

Ideas That Can Get You Down

Unfortunately, GLBTQ people often are not treated equally in our society. Homophobia and transphobia may take the form of overt harassment. Prejudice can also appear in more subtle forms. It's important to recognize when this kind of negativity starts to take a toll on you. Here are some common thoughts that can lead to depression and some words of reassurance that can help you remember that you are fine just the way you are.

I am the only GLBTQ person in the entire world. Feeling like you're the only one can really bring you down. It can help to remember that commonly accepted statistics suggest that roughly one out of every ten people is GLBTQ. With billions of people in this world, that's a whole lot of queer folks.

BEEN THERE

"I had my youth group to go to every Tuesday night when I was in high school. I had three adults to talk to if I ever needed something from them, and I had the whole group. We would discuss our problems and get advice from each other on what we could do to help our situations." —Ivana, 19

There is something wrong with being GLBTQ. Maybe because you've heard that it's wrong to be GLBTQ for so long that part of you is starting to believe it. Many teens worry that it's bad to be queer. But being GLBTQ is completely natural. It doesn't make you wrong or bad or mentally ill. A lot of medical and mental health groups say the same thing. Here are just a few:

- American Academy of Pediatrics
- American Counseling Association
- American Psychiatric Association
- National Association of School Psychologists
- National Association of Social Workers

These groups collectively represent about half a million health and mental health professionals. They all maintain that queerness is not a mental disorder and it's not wrong to be GLBTQ.

I can never have a normal life. GLBTQ people can live the most "normal" of lives—no matter what your definition of that word might be. We can be doctors, lawyers, politicians, construction workers, artists, teachers, parents, counselors, clergy, executives, military service members, business owners, factory workers . . . anything we want to be. We can have families. We can own homes. In our lifetimes, we experience joys and sorrows, love and heartbreak, pleasure and pain just like anyone else.

I'm popular and I have friends. I *should* be happy, but I'm not. Even if you have great friends, get good grades, and have a great family, that doesn't necessarily mean that your life is easy. When you are trying to understand your sexual orientation or gender identity, you can feel like you're alone and out of sync with the rest of the world—even if everything looks good from the outside. And while occasionally feeling blue is normal, speak with an adult at home or at school right away if you feel this way a lot of the time.

Most mental health experts agree that the source of some people's depression has little to do with outside factors. Instead, their depression is related to imbalances in the chemicals in the brain that regulate their moods. Some people may be more prone to depression if it runs in their family. Speak with a mental health professional to help you figure out the source of your depression.

Everybody hates me because I'm GLBTQ. It might feel like that at times, but the truth is a lot of people care about you. For many people, it probably doesn't matter whether you're queer or straight. The following numbers might give you a more positive perspective.

According to GLSEN research:

- In the United States, 80 percent of parents favor expanding existing antiharassment and antidiscrimination policies to include queer students
- 80 percent of parents also support teacher sensitivity training on tolerance that includes instructions on dealing with harassment of GLBTQ students in schools
- 63 percent of parents favor including positive information about gay and lesbian people in middle and high school health and sex education classes, and 60 percent also favor including positive information about transgender people in those forums

According to the Pew Research Center for People and the Press, public acceptance of homosexuality has increased in a number of ways in recent years:

- Opposition to gay marriage has fallen across the board, with substantial declines among both Democrats and Republicans
- 46 percent of those surveyed support gay and lesbian adoption (up from 38 percent in 1999)

Warning Signs of Depression

It's important to be aware of what's going on with your emotions, especially if you notice that you're feeling sad or upset more of the time. Even though family members and friends care for you and want to be sure you're healthy, they might not notice the kinds of changes that can signal depression. Depression is a serious condition in which people experience extreme feelings of sadness or hopelessness. These moods are more severe and last longer than the typical ups and downs of adolescence and can have a big impact on how teens behave. Experiencing any of the following symptoms for more than two weeks may be a sign you are depressed:

Emotional changes:

- ☐ anger
- ☐ guilt
- ☐ anxiety
- ☐ feeling emotional numbness
- ☐ feeling hopeless
- ☐ irritability
- ☐ indifference
- ☐ loneliness
- ☐ sadness
- ☐ bitterness
- ☐ feeling worthless
- ☐ feeling helpless
- ☐ loss of motivation

Physical changes:

- ☐ sleeping problems (too much or too little)
- ☐ overeating or loss of appetite (often with weight gain or weight loss)
- ☐ headaches
- ☐ indigestion, stomachaches, or nausea
- ☐ aches or pains for unknown reasons
- ☐ fatigue or lack of energy

Changes in thought:

- ☐ difficulty remembering or concentrating
- ☐ confusion
- ☐ believing that no one cares about you
- ☐ loss of interest in things you used to enjoy
- ☐ pessimism (negative thinking about things)
- ☐ believing that you don't deserve to be happy
- ☐ believing that you're a burden to others
- ☐ blaming yourself for anything that goes wrong
- ☐ thoughts racing through your head
- ☐ thoughts of harming yourself
- ☐ thoughts of death or suicide

▼ **Get Help!** If you're feeling suicidal or thinking about hurting yourself, it's important to talk with someone *right away*. If there isn't a trusted adult or friend you can go to, contact one of these hotlines. They can provide immediate support and connect you with additional resources in your area. It takes a strong person to ask for help, and we all need someone to lean on now and then.

The Trevor Lifeline (1-866-4-U-TREVOR/1-866-488-7386). The Trevor Lifeline is a 24-hour toll-free suicide hotline for GLBTQ teens staffed by highly trained counselors. Check out the website at www.thetrevorproject.org for information about how to help someone who is suicidal, as well as for support groups and resources for GLBTQ teens.

Boys Town National Hotline (1-800-448-3000). This crisis hotline for both girls and boys is available 24 hours a day. Professional counselors listen and offer advice on any issue, including depression, suicide, and identity struggles.

National Runaway Switchboard (1-800-RUNAWAY/1-800-786-2929). This hotline for teens in crisis is staffed 24 hours a day by counselors who will listen to you and help you build a plan of action to address whatever problems you're having.

Remember, there's nothing wrong with asking for help. It doesn't mean something is wrong with you, just that something is wrong in your life right now. Being depressed can make it hard to maintain perspective. That's why it's important to get support from an outsider who can help you sort through your feelings. ▼

Changes in behavior:

- ☐ aggression
- ☐ moving and talking more slowly
- ☐ poor hygiene
- ☐ acting out (skipping school, unsafe driving, running away, taking part in risky sexual behaviors)
- ☐ using/abusing drugs (including alcohol and nicotine)
- ☐ crying more than usual
- ☐ underachieving or overachieving
- ☐ spending most of your time alone and withdrawing from friends or family, or fear of being alone
- ☐ hurting yourself (such as cutting, bruising, or burning yourself)

The previous checklists were adapted from *When Nothing Matters Anymore* by Bev Cobain, an excellent resource for young people going through depression (see page 207).

Making a Deal for Life

Make a deal with a trusted friend or family member. If you're ever feeling really low, you can call him and he'll be there for you any time you need to talk. Likewise, promise you'll be there for him, too. You might never end up needing to call him in the middle of the night, but it can make you feel better to know you always have someone to lean on.

We, [insert your name] and [insert your friend's name], hereby swear that we will henceforth, from here on out and into infinity, be there for one another. We know that, at any hour of the day or night, if we really need to talk, we can call and the other will listen. Also, we swear that if we ever have thoughts of doing ourselves harm, we will call the other person for help.

Signed:

Person #1 _____

Date _____

Person #2 _____

Date _____

Thinking About Drinking:
Making Decisions About Alcohol

Being a teen means making a lot of tough decisions about alcohol, nicotine, and other drugs. It's your body, and those choices are yours to make. You'll have to live with the outcomes, so it's in your best interest to make the most informed decisions possible.

While overall use of alcohol, drugs, and tobacco has declined somewhat for teens in the last several years, overall substance abuse rates are still much higher for GLBTQ teens than for their straight peers. A 2008 article published in the journal *Addiction,* which analyzed data from 18 different studies conducted between 1994 and 2006, reported that GLBTQ teens are 190 percent more likely than heterosexual teens to use drugs or alcohol. The numbers are even higher among subgroups. For example, bisexual teens are 340 percent more likely to use drugs or alcohol than straight peers, and lesbians are 400 percent more likely.

Why are these numbers so high? Dr. Michael Marshal, a researcher from the University of Pittsburgh and the main author of the study, said, "Homophobia, discrimination, and victimization are largely responsible for these substance use disparities in young gay people." Still, he noted, "It is important to remember that the vast majority of gay youth are happy and healthy, despite the stressors of living in a . . . homophobic society."

Realizing and accepting that you're GLBTQ can be incredibly stressful, especially when it's combined with the general everyday stresses of being a teenager. The verbal and sometimes physical harassment that many queer teens deal with can increase stress levels, too. That stress can contribute to depression, which may lead to substance use. Many teens looking to escape stress and worries turn to alcohol and drugs, thinking those will cheer them up, mellow them out, help them fit in, or numb them to issues they're dealing with.

BEEN THERE

"Drugs and alcohol can be a problem for many GLBTQ men and women. It makes us feel temporarily like our problems are gone and life is great. But the truth is the more you do, the worse you feel. Life just gets worse. Relationships fall apart and people get hurt."
—Ben, 18

A Gay Old Time? The Party Scene in GLBTQ Life

Some people believe the stereotypes that all or most GLBTQ people drink, smoke, and use drugs. While the bar and club scene does have a place in GLBTQ culture, the idea that all queer people party and use drugs and alcohol is far from true.

In an interview with GayHealth.com, Michele Fitzsimmons, outreach coordinator for the Lesbian AIDS Project, said that GLBTQ teens tend to gravitate toward queer bars and clubs because they're some of the only places teens feel comfortable expressing their sexuality. "When you're coming out, your self-esteem might be shaky," Michele says. "It's very easy to slip into a situation where [drug and alcohol use] becomes an addiction or that use puts the user at risk."

Bars and clubs aren't supposed to admit people under 21, but many teens still sneak in illegally. Unfortunately, the bar and club scene can be dangerous. People desperate for acceptance may drink to fit in or smoke to strike up a conversation. Others might take ecstasy or crystal meth to boost their confidence or feel relaxed. If you find yourself in a club tempted to try these substances, remember the effects they can have on you. And remember, not all GLBTQ people in clubs drink, smoke, or use drugs. It's definitely not a requirement to fit in.

Being in a bar or club requires staying alert. Many people in clubs aren't thinking clearly or using good judgment because they've been drinking or using drugs. Others may be sober but looking to harm or take advantage of people. So be smart. For example, if you want something to drink, get it yourself. Don't let someone you don't know very well bring you any kind of drink— even bottled water. No matter how nice she might seem, she could easily slip GHB (G), ketamine (Special K), Rohypnol (roofie), or another substance into it. If you're under 21, it's illegal to be in a bar or club, so even if you don't use drugs or alcohol, just being in these establishments can lead to severe consequences that have a negative impact on your life.

The Truth About Drinking

In the United States, turning 21 is considered a huge rite of passage. Many young people look forward to being able to legally drink. Many teens can't wait to try alcohol. But amid all this excitement, it's easy to forget that alcohol is a drug that can cause a lot of problems. Many people—not just teens—have misconceptions about how alcohol affects the body.

Here are some common myths:

When you're feeling stressed or depressed, having a drink will make things better. How many times have we heard people exclaim, "I need a drink!" after a tough day? GLBTQ teens do have a lot to deal with, but alcohol won't help you forget bad feelings or problems. In fact, it can compound them. Alcohol is a depressant that slows down your brain. Drinking it can contribute to depressed feelings and prevent you from thinking clearly. While it might seem like alcohol is giving you a lift, it's actually bringing you down. Alcohol use can also negatively impact the quality and duration of sleep, which can negatively affect your body and intensify feelings of depression.

Drinking makes you look cool or mature. For GLBTQ teens, the idea that drinking can help them fit in—whether they're at a high school party or a 21-and-over club—can be attractive. But alcohol won't suddenly make someone popular or fit in. In fact, underage drinking can cause you to behave around others in ways that you later regret. It also can give people the wrong impression about you and what's important to you.

Drinking will help you meet people. Maybe you think having a drink or two will help you relax and be more social, but meeting people while under the influence of alcohol or other drugs is not the way to put your best foot forward. If you're looking for meaningful relationships and new friends, you won't come across as your best self if you're tipsy or flat-out drunk. You could say or do embarrassing things—things you'd never do or say when you're sober. Or you might end up making decisions about things like sexual contact or drinking and driving that you later regret.

BEEN THERE

"During the nine months that I was drinking, I didn't meet one person who I knew was gay. Once I could stop drinking, I made several gay friends and, ultimately, started to date again. Although I came out to my father and to all my friends when I was 16, it was almost like coming out again once I stopped drinking. I met a lot of new people and came to terms again with who I am." —Blake, 20

Ways to Say No to Alcohol

By refusing to drink, you're looking out for yourself and showing confidence in who you are. What's more, you can say no to drinking without feeling awkward, self-conscious, or like a prude. Here are some tips for turning down alcohol, even when others are pressuring you.

- Order a drink, but buy club soda and lime or something else nonalcoholic. Just holding a nonalcoholic drink may help you feel more comfortable.
- If someone asks you if you want a drink, say, "No, thanks," or hold up your cranberry juice and say, "I've got one," or say "I'd rather go dance."
- Be a designated driver. At some clubs, designated drivers get unlimited free nonalcoholic drinks.
- If someone brings you a drink anyway, you don't have to accept it. Again, hold up your soda and say, "Thanks, but I'm good." A real friend's not going to pressure you to drink.
- Be supportive of friends who choose not to drink.

Getting Help for Addiction

Association of Lesbian, Gay, Bisexual and Transgender Addiction Professionals and Their Allies (www.nalgap.org). This organization is devoted to preventing and treating addiction in the GLBTQ community. Visit the site for information on the devastating effects of drug and alcohol abuse or to seek a referral for treatment.

National Council on Alcoholism and Drug Dependence (www.ncadd.org). Visit this site for information on drug and alcohol addiction as well as resources for support. Or you can call 1-800-622-2255 for local treatment referrals.

The Truth About Tobacco

Did you know that GLBTQ teens are more likely than their straight peers to use tobacco? A study published in the *Archives of Pediatric and Adolescent Medicine* showed that gay, lesbian, and bisexual teens reported much higher use of cigarettes and smokeless tobacco than heterosexual teens.

A National Youth Advocacy Coalition report released in 2010 also examined smoking among GLBTQ teens. The report showed that unique stressors, such as discrimination and lack of family acceptance, contributed to higher rates of tobacco use. It also revealed that many queer young people see smoking as an important social activity. In fact, of the teens surveyed, only

28 percent reported having never smoked. The average age at which respondents began smoking was 15.

For decades, the tobacco industry—a group of companies that makes their money from getting people addicted to something that can and does kill—has used ads, product placements, and other messaging vehicles to convince us that smoking is cool and will improve the quality of our lives. Some of this advertising has been aimed directly at young and queer people. Think about who they're targeting—*you*.

Documents from the tobacco industry that have been made public consistently show Big Tobacco targets teens with its marketing messages. Big Tobacco also targeted queer people in the 1990s with a marketing project called Project Subculture Urban Marketing, known inside the major tobacco company R.J. Reynolds as Project SCUM. Are those the kinds of companies you want to support?

Getting Hooked on Tobacco

If you're feeling isolated or eager to meet others, smoking can seem like a good social link or a way to approach others. Some people like to use lines like, "Got a light?" or "Can I bum a smoke?" when they want to meet someone.

Nicotine, a powerful and addictive chemical in tobacco, can make smoking easy to start but hard to stop. It provides smokers with a rush that can feel very satisfying—many people are hooked at once. Studies show it is more addictive than heroin. Nicotine cravings can be so intense that people are willing to stand outside in pouring rain or subzero weather to get their fix. If you doubt how tough it can be to quit, just think about how many advertisements you see for stop-smoking programs, gums, patches, and pills.

GLBTQ teens sometimes turn to smoking for a release from daily stresses. These young people use smoking as a way to relax or relieve some of the depressed feelings they might have. Tobacco might give them a temporary feeling of relief, but it's just that—temporary. And it comes at a steep cost—increased heart rate, decreased stamina, decreased lung capacity, and increased risk of developing cancer. That's not to mention the price of cigarettes or the unavoidable foul-smelling breath, clothes, and hair.

If you're still not convinced that smoking is bad for you, consider this:

According to the Centers for Disease Control, tobacco is one of the biggest causes of preventable and premature death in the United States, claiming the lives of more than 440,000 people each year. And roughly 90 percent of cigarette smokers become addicted before the age of 19.

Avoiding Drugs

Just as with alcohol and tobacco, GLBTQ teens have higher rates of drug use than their straight peers do. It's not that queer teens are fundamentally prone to substance abuse. It all comes down to stress and depressed feelings. Some GLBTQ teens desperately want to feel better, and they think using drugs will help them relax and fit in with others. In the end, drugs don't work any better than drinking or smoking. They won't improve your life or help you feel good about who you are.

BEEN THERE

"I started doing drugs when I was nine. I tried to fit in with that crowd and hide my 'secret identity.' By the time I was 13, I was put in drug rehab. . . . My rehab counselor told me I wasn't going to be able to stop using unless I was true to myself. I went home and thought about what he said. The next day I started coming out to friends." —Sam, 15

Instead of solving problems, drugs compound them. When you're feeling depressed, drugs make you feel a little better at first, but then, as the effects wear off, much worse (similar to the effects of alcohol). Some drugs can make you feel like you're stuck in a bottomless pit or out of control. If you're feeling stressed, drugs that are supposed to make you happy often leave you feeling paranoid, jittery, or out of control. In general, drugs are unpredictable. You don't really know what you're getting, and you can't be sure how they're going to make you feel.

If you like to go out dancing or to raves, it's likely you'll come across drugs like crystal meth, ecstasy, ketamine, marijuana, or GHB. These so-called club drugs can be just as dangerous and unpredictable as any other drugs. It can be tempting to think they'll help you forget about the teasing at school or the fight you had with your parents about your girlfriend, or that they'll make it easier to let go and party. It doesn't work that way. Drug use always has consequences, whether or not they're immediately apparent. Not only do drugs damage your body and your judgment, they're also illegal and could get you in trouble with the law.

Even if you're not using drugs yourself, someone else's drug use could get you into serious trouble. Never ride with someone who is drunk or high, even if she swears to you that she's sober. If you have a license, offer to drive her somewhere. But even if she refuses, don't get in the car with her. If you do, you're putting your life in her hands.

Educate Yourself

Partnership for a Drug-Free America (www.drugfreeamerica.org). Visit this website to find out more about specific drugs and their effects. The site includes the real stories of teens who used drugs and paid the consequences.

The Truth (www.thetruth.com). Visit this site to learn about the real health effects tobacco has on your body and about the marketing practices the tobacco industry uses to promote smoking among teens.

▼ **"But it's just pot."** Sound familiar? Marijuana has a misleading reputation of being virtually harmless. But pot is a drug that impairs your thinking and judgment (not to mention your lungs). According to the National Institute on Drug Abuse, which conducts scientific studies on how drugs affect the brain, "Marijuana intoxication can cause distorted perceptions, impaired coordination, difficulty in thinking and problem solving, and problems with learning and memory. Research has shown that marijuana's adverse impact on learning and memory can last for days or weeks after the acute effects of the drug wear off. . . . Research on the long-term effects of marijuana abuse indicates some changes in the brain similar to those seen after long-term abuse of other major drugs." That doesn't sound very good. And, with the exception of medical use laws in a few states, marijuana is illegal. Using it can lead to some very serious consequences. ▼

The fact is no chemically induced high comes without a hitch. For anything drugs give you, they take away something else. And what they take is a lot more valuable to you in the long run than the high they give you in the short run. Some teens stay away from so-called club drugs, but try diet pills or performance-enhancing drugs. The rule still applies even if the substance is herbal. Drug use comes with consequences, some of which are life threatening.

No matter what anyone tells you or how badly you might sometimes feel, you have the potential to make anything you want of your life. You can do amazing things. If you need help getting through a rough spot, reach out for it. It's there and it's never too late.

BEEN THERE

"I remember shooting up a mixture of heroin and cocaine, and what happened next really scared me to the point of not wanting to touch drugs and alcohol again. I was 20 and I was down on my knees in the middle of the night, blood pouring out of my nose, throwing up. I just remember praying that if I woke from this that I would never touch drugs again. I was very lucky during that time I was using drugs that I didn't catch anything, that I wasn't raped, or that I didn't kill anyone else or myself." —Xian, 26

Getting Clean as a GLBTQ Teen (and Staying That Way!)

If you're using drugs, alcohol, or tobacco, quitting could be one of the most difficult things you ever do in your life, especially if you're still coming to terms with being GLBTQ. Even though it's challenging, getting clean will also be one of the most positive things you can do. It's a crucial step to getting yourself back on track.

No matter what forces are working against you (your dad can't accept that you're queer, you're being harassed at school, you're feeling isolated), you do have the power to change your life. No matter what's going on outside of you, a whole lot of strength exists inside you. You *can* stay sober.

Here's some advice on how to get and stay sober:

Recognize that you have a problem. Is it hard or even impossible for you to function without drugs, alcohol, or tobacco? Be honest. If you don't see a problem, you can't solve it.

Get help. The support of your family members, friends, doctor, or counselor can be of great help when you quit using. If you don't feel you can approach a parent about your substance use, seek the support of another adult you trust. Talk with your guidance counselor, your favorite teacher, a relative, a religious leader, a doctor, or another caring adult. It's important that someone—an adult—knows about your problem and can be there to help. This can be tough because it probably will involve you coming out to the person you talk with, but you can do it. You're worth it.

Remember why you're trying to quit. Getting sober won't be easy. It helps, though, to remember the benefits of overcoming addiction. You'll feel better both physically and mentally. And conquering drugs and alcohol will make you a stronger person than you probably thought you could be.

After you've stopped drinking or taking drugs, it can be hard to stay off them. Here are some things that might help you:

Once you start a treatment program, tell your friends about your decision to stop using drugs. Your true friends will respect and support your decision. It is possible that you'll have to find a new group of friends who are completely supportive of your efforts to stay sober. Avoid hanging around people you used to do drugs, drink, or smoke with if they continue to use. It can be very easy to fall back into old habits and behaviors.

Let your friends and family know how important their support is and ask them to be there for you when you need them. It's important that you have someone you can call in the middle of the night if you need to talk. Even if you don't end up calling, knowing someone is there can help a lot.

Only accept invitations to events that you know (or are at least reasonably certain) won't involve drinking or drugs. Especially when you're first recovering, it's safer to avoid situations in which you may be tempted to use.

Plan in advance what you'll do in situations where alcohol or drugs are around. You'll likely be tempted to start using or drinking again, but knowing beforehand how you'll approach difficult situations can make them easier to deal with. Your plan might be as simple as "get the heck out of there." Even so, if you know in advance what you'll do, it's easier to follow through and take care of yourself when you need to.

Always remember that having an addiction doesn't make you a bad or weak person. If you slip up in your efforts to stay clean, get help as soon as possible. But remember how difficult what you're doing is and know that there's nothing to be ashamed of. You can get back on track. You've made a lot of positive changes in your life and one lapse doesn't change that.

BEEN THERE

"As I complete six years clean and sober, I have just begun finding out who I really am. Now I find myself surrounded by men and women whose friendship I am thankful for every day." —Lee, 26

Issues like homophobia and ignorance about gender identity are things that you sometimes have little or no control over. Focusing on things you can control, such as adopting positive and healthy behaviors, goes a long way toward creating a happier and more fulfilling life for yourself.

Chapter 9
Religion and Culture

You are a mosaic.

Many different aspects make up who you are as a person. Sexuality is an important part of the whole, but religion, culture, and ethnicity also play a role in your day-to-day life. They can influence your priorities, how you see yourself, and how you relate to others in society. If you were raised with strong religious or cultural beliefs, coming to terms with your gender identity or sexual orientation might leave you feeling confused about who you are or your place in the world.

Some people have trouble accepting themselves as GLBTQ, or they have trouble gaining acceptance from loved ones, because of religious beliefs and cultural traditions. The roots of religion and culture can run very deep, and anything that challenges those beliefs can be met with resistance and even anger. This might make it hard to understand yourself or for others, such as family and friends, to understand you. Accepting yourself and coming out is even more stressful if you feel that you have to choose between your cultural or ethnic identity and being GLBTQ.

Religion and culture sometimes are difficult to separate as influences because religion can play a key role in defining the beliefs and traditions common to a culture. For example, Catholicism is often an integral part of Latino and Filipino cultures. Islam is influential in cultures around the world from the Middle East to parts of Asia, the Pacific Rim, and even America. The Christian faith often is considered to be a cornerstone of African-American culture.

In this chapter, *congregation* is used to mean a gathering of people for the purpose of religious worship or instruction. It is not used to imply a reference to a specific faith. Also, it is used interchangeably with *religious community, faith community,* and *place of worship.*

If your religion teaches that it's wrong to be GLBTQ, that belief might surface throughout the culture, not just inside the temple, church, or mosque. It's not surprising that you could find yourself with conflicted emotions. On one hand, you want to come to terms with your sexuality and accept yourself. On the other hand, you've grown up as a part of a religion or culture that teaches that who you are is not okay. So now what?

States of Being: Religious Life and GLBTQ Life

For some families with GLBTQ loved ones, religion can be a huge challenge to reconcile. For others, it's not an issue at all, either because they do not observe a religion or their religion or faith is inclusive and openly accepting of GLBTQ people. Then there are those in the middle—queer people whose families accept them, but their religions do not.

Religion is important in many people's lives and that might be true for you, too. In the United States and many other countries, it's very common to grow up in a family that practices some kind of organized religion. According to several Gallup polls conducted in 2008, 77 percent of Americans identify as some form of Christian (this includes both Protestants and Catholics). Slightly greater than 1 percent identified as Jewish and slightly less than 1 percent identified as "other," which includes Muslim,

Buddhist, Hindu, and other religions. Additionally, 12 percent of Americans reported no religious identity.

On the surface, religion and sexuality don't seem to have much to do with each other. Being GLBTQ is about your sexual orientation or gender identity—the result of a combination of biological and emotional factors. Religion is about spiritual beliefs. So why is religion such a complicated and even painful issue for many GLBTQ people?

A History Lesson

Many major religions have difficulty accepting or finding a place for their GLBTQ members for various reasons. They can be scriptural, historical, rooted in cultural traditions that have become part of religious beliefs, or a combination of these.

For example, some religions believe that a union between a man and a woman is sacred either because it is stated or they *interpret* that it is stated in scripture. A strong, positive, and loving relationship between two people is definitely something to celebrate. However, the idea that the union between a man and a woman is sacred is often held because the couple can reproduce without scientific intervention. In fact, some religions believe that a couple should have sexual intercourse only for the purpose of reproduction—not for pleasure—and that the use of contraception is immoral. As a result of such beliefs, GLBTQ people can find themselves, their sexuality, and their relationships rejected by their religion because reproduction isn't the primary purpose of their romantic and physical relationships.

A Powerful Documentary

Out in the Silence. This touching documentary chronicles a gay filmmaker's journey from Washington, D.C., back to his small Pennsylvania hometown, where he explores the roots of the homophobia dividing the town. The film also focuses on C.J., an out 16-year-old who has withdrawn from the local school because of escalating harassment. This open-minded film shows a broad variety of perspectives with much of the discussion centering on religion. With understanding and dialogue, minds can indeed change. The documentary is available on DVD (www.wpsu.org/outinthesilence).

▼ A Research Project If you want to find out more about your religion's history but aren't sure where to start, an Internet or a library search could be a good jumping-off point. If you feel comfortable doing so, approach a religious leader in your community and ask for recommendations, or your congregation might have its own library. Some of these sources might be biased—consider who the author is when making your assessment—but some of them could provide solid historical information. Also, many queer-positive religious organizations (see pages 156–157) have suggested resources and reading lists. ▼

Encouraging Open Minds: Starting a Dialogue

Knowledge can be your best path to finding acceptance and understanding in your religious community. When people start looking at where their personal beliefs and their religion's beliefs come from, it can get them thinking. The question, "Why do we believe this?" might seem simple, but people can be afraid to explore or challenge their own belief systems. Often they're afraid that what they could discover about some of their beliefs might end up invalidating all of them.

If you're struggling with your religion, find out about its history and where anti-GLBTQ beliefs might have originated. Read the original writings or scriptures to get a better idea of how others have interpreted them. An issue or idea can be taken out of context and personal opinions can influence interpretations. And something that is supposedly expressly stated in scripture might not be unequivocal after all.

If you have a loved one who's struggling with her religion and anti-GLBTQ beliefs, talk with her about what you've learned. She might not be willing to listen, or she might sit down and really consider the information. Investigating your religion's roots and starting a dialogue are positive steps toward reconciling who you are with your religious beliefs. If you're at a loss as to how to approach family, friends, or people in your religious community, refer back to the coming out information in Chapter 3 (beginning on page 48) for tips on effective communication. Much of that advice is appropriate for approaching a wide variety of topics that can be difficult to discuss.

Room for Change

Many religious communities are engaged in debates about their queer members. These debates might include whether or not to accept GLBTQ members, specific conditions under which GLBTQ members are allowed to be part of the congregation, and whether or not to perform same-sex marriage or commitment ceremonies. While some religions might never accept GLBTQ people, many are finally thinking and talking about it. That's where change begins. Even when religious leaders decide not to accept GLBTQ people, debates over the issue can help open and change individuals' minds. Several individual congregations have declared themselves open and accepting of queer people.

It can be very discouraging to hear that a group of religious leaders has officially decided not to welcome GLBTQ people. Don't think about this in terms of an entire denomination or congregation, because within any group, some of the people will disagree and accept queer people.

Gay Religious Leaders: Changing Views Within Religious Communities

Many religious groups have or are taking part in debates about whether leadership roles can be filled by gays and/or lesbians. (Some of these religions still do not allow women, whether straight or gay, to hold leadership roles.) On July 8, 2010, leaders in the Presbyterian Church voted to allow non-celibate gay people in committed relationships to serve as clergy. Previously, all clergy, deacons, and elders had to be married or celibate.

The Episcopal denomination has also made great strides in GLBTQ acceptance. It not only allows openly gay people to serve as priests, but also allows them to become bishops.

The debate in the Catholic Church over allowing openly gay priests is ongoing, though one alternative Catholic denomination—the North American Old Catholic Church—has already ordained several priests who are openly gay.

The Jewish community has both openly gay rabbis and openly gay Orthodox rabbis. In August 2010, 150 Orthodox Jewish rabbis signed a statement of acceptance toward gays and lesbians practicing in their faith. The statement read in part, "Jews with homosexual orientations or same-sex attractions should be welcomed as full members of the synagogue and school community."

Making Room in Religion: Reconciling Your Personal Beliefs

Religion and culture can be very personal, meaningful aspects of a person's life, and that doesn't have to change because you're queer. You might find a place for yourself in your religion or in a different spiritual tradition. Or you could follow your spiritual beliefs as an individual rather than as part of a group. You might even connect with other like-minded individuals and create your own community online.

BEEN THERE

"I don't consider myself as having a religious background because organized religion is not the way for me to go. I consider myself a very spiritual person without the aspect of religion. Religion doesn't affect me either way, at least not on a level I notice. I know that learning that I'm GLBTQ would affect my family very negatively. They can't see beyond the religion." —Li, 20

Here are some common questions and answers that might help you figure out what's best for you right now:

Q: What do I do if my place of worship doesn't accept GLBTQ people?
A: First, are you sure that queer people aren't welcome at your place of worship, or have you made that assumption on your own? Have you been taught that it's wrong to be GLBTQ, or do you assume your congregation isn't accepting either because

nothing has been said about it or because you don't know of any other GLBTQ members?

Whatever the case, you might want to approach the leader of your congregation to explore her views on having GLBTQ members. If one or both of your parents is accepting, perhaps they could accompany you. Your religious leader might be willing to explore the issue with you, and the two of you can grow together. Then, perhaps the entire congregation could move toward becoming more open and accepting.

Just as accepting yourself and coming out is a process, so is change. Give your religious leader and community a chance. Several national organizations have members who are willing to visit places of worship to talk with faith leaders or congregations about becoming more open and accepting.

▼ GLBTQ-Positive Religious Organizations

Affirmation (www.affirmation.org). This organization supports GLBTQ Mormons and their families and friends. The group's website has separate sections for youth, women, and people who are transgender.

Al-Fatiha (www.al-fatiha.org). Al-Fatiha is dedicated to Muslims of all cultural and ethnic backgrounds who are gay, lesbian, bisexual, transgender, intersex, or questioning. The organization's website features a community space and resource center.

DignityUSA (www.dignityusa.org). An organization supporting queer Catholics and their families and friends, DignityUSA has a website that features topic-specific online discussion groups. Also available are teen resources and links to local chapters.

Gay Christian Network (www.gaychristian.net). This ministry serves GLBTQ Christians and those who care about them. Their site includes audio and video files of sermons, testimonies, and message boards. Also check out the documentary *Through My Eyes,* which features over two dozen young gay Christians discussing their journeys to reconcile their faith and sexuality.

Gay Jews (http://djs28.tripod.com). This is a site for GLBTQ Orthodox Jews. It includes a forum, online bookstore, chat room, and links to other resources for queer Jews.

Q: What if my religious community won't accept me?

A: Unfortunately, some religious communities and congregations won't be willing to change. But even if yours is one of them, don't assume that you will be forced to abandon your religion. You might be surprised to learn that, in almost every religion, some branches or denominations accept GLBTQ people. This is because the key religious texts (for example the Bible, Torah, or Koran) are interpreted in a variety of ways. Some interpretations are more conservative, others are more liberal and inclusive. Your particular place of worship might welcome only straight people, but another congregation within your faith might be more open and accepting.

How welcoming or open a place of worship is to queer people can depend on a number of different factors: where you live, the congregation's familiarity with GLBTQ people, how diverse

Integrity (www.integrityusa.org). Integrity is a nonprofit organization supporting queer Episcopalians and advocating for their full inclusion in the Episcopal Church. The group's website contains resources, links to local chapters, and information about how to get involved.

Interfaith Alliance (www.interfaithalliance.org). A nonpartisan, clergy-led grassroots organization, Interfaith Alliance is dedicated to protecting religious freedom and promoting common ground among religions. The group is active in lobbying for GLBTQ civil rights.

JQ Youth (www.jqyouth.org). This site is for GLBTQ Jews ages 17–30. Check it out to find links to books and other resources, stories from young queer Jews, and discussion groups.

Soulforce (www.soulforce.org). Soulforce is an interfaith group that applies principles of nonviolence to stopping inflammatory or false information about GLBTQ people. Resources at the organization's website include publications, videos, information on interpretations of religious texts, an online community center, and information on how to become involved in advocacy efforts.

Metropolitan Community Churches (www.ufmcc.com). Metropolitan Community Churches have for decades been places where GLBTQ people can worship. The organization also has a long history of advocating for queer rights. Visit the site for online classes, discussions of Bible passages often used against GLBTQ people, and other resources. ▼

the congregation is, the individual beliefs of the community's spiritual leader, and so on.

Some people choose to stay with their original congregation, but continue to work for change. Others opt to stay in their congregation and reconcile themselves to the idea that the faith community won't change. There is no right or wrong decision. Religion is a very personal issue and only you can decide what's best for you.

BEEN THERE

"I'm Lutheran. Some people might not realize that there are basically two different Lutheran churches — the Evangelical Lutheran Church of America (ELCA) and the Lutheran Church, Missouri Synod (LCMS). One is very liberal, and the other is more hellfire and damnation. There is a push in the ELCA church to allow GLBTQ pastors in committed relationships to be ordained. In the past, you could only be ordained if you were straight or, as a GLBTQ person, chose celibacy. There are those who grew up LCMS, like my mother, who are not so accepting." —Charlotte, 19

You might be in a situation that for now makes it difficult or impossible for you to attend a different place of worship. Maybe you're too young to drive or you simply don't have access to transportation. For these or other reasons, you might have to wait a while to make changes.

Remember, nothing is wrong with you. You deserve as many opportunities and as much happiness as anyone else in the world. Continue to explore your religion and look for ways to find your place in it despite the views of your congregation or religious leader.

Q: What if I can't find another congregation within my religion that is open and accepting?

A: You might be able to find a different denomination, or branch, within your religion that holds similar beliefs and has a more accepting congregation in your area. For example, Christianity has many denominations. They all work within the same basic belief system and use the Bible as their religious text, but they might have different interpretations, views, and practices. Some denominations have a lot in common, some less. You might be able to find a congregation within a similar denomination that would be comfortable for you.

If no other denomination is similar to yours, or an accepting faith community within a similar denomination isn't close to you, you might have to look at other options. You may even decide to consider joining a completely different denomination or exploring other spiritual practices and traditions.

Some spiritual communities, such as the Unitarian Universalists, welcome everyone. These communities might have within the same congregation members who are Jewish, Buddhist, Muslim, Christian, or Wiccan, or members who don't subscribe to a particular religious focus at all. The worship services are conducted in such a way that all beliefs are respected. While this could be a big change from the way you're used to worshipping, you can always visit to see what you think. You might love it and decide to stay, or you might feel that it's not the right choice for you.

Q: None of these options works for me. What can I do?

A: You *still* have more options. Some GLBTQ people decide that they can't, at least at this point in their lives, reconcile their sexual orientation or gender identity with organized religion. While the prospect might be scary for you if you've grown up with a strong religious background, it might help

Resources for Queer Christians

Roughly 77 percent of Americans self-identify as Christian. The resources below specifically address issues of homosexuality and the Bible.

What the Bible Really Says About Homosexuality by Daniel Helminiak. Written by a Roman Catholic priest, this book provides commentary on biblical passages. The author concludes that the Bible supplies no real basis for the condemnation of homosexuality.

Jesus, the Bible, and Homosexuality by Jack Rogers. A professor of theology, Rogers provides a discussion of GLBTQ issues in Christianity. His primary argument is that being queer and Christian are not mutually exclusive.

For the Bible Tells Me So. This documentary is about the conflict between Christian fundamentalism and homosexuality. In the film, real families discuss their experiences (www.forthebibletellsmeso.org).

Through My Eyes. See page 156.

to remember that religion is about exploration. Give yourself the opportunity to explore what is right for you.

You might look into other religious traditions and find one that's more accepting and feels like a better fit. You could move to a new denomination, or you could eventually end up some place where you find an accepting religious community in your original denomination. You might also opt to practice your religion on your own. Observing your faith or exploring your spirituality in a more personal way (outside of a formal setting) may help you clarify what you believe.

Remember, whatever decision you make now doesn't have to be permanent. You can change your mind. You might decide that you need to leave organized religion—for a short period or for longer. In the meantime, you could maintain your religious practices or explore your spiritual beliefs as an individual. Or maybe you'll eventually decide that religion doesn't have a place in your life at all.

BEEN THERE

"Around 14 or 15, I got deeply religious and bought myself a Bible. I began attending church regularly and went to study groups and nightly Bible classes. I suppose I was trying to make it work, since everyone assumed I would get into it if I just tried harder. But in the end, it just never worked. It wasn't for me. When I think about the specifics, it's like everything I do and the things I like are all wrong so that I'm bad. But I'm not! I'm not bad, so the problem is elsewhere. Since then, I've explored a number of different religions and spiritualities." —Orlando, 19

The decision to leave organized religion, change religions, or practice on your own might be upsetting to your family. Talking to them about it calmly and rationally might help, especially if you explain how and why you made your decision. You could choose to add that you're not closing yourself off to religion, you're just taking another path, at least for now. You might come back, you might not.

Some parents or guardians respect such decisions (even if they don't like them). Others do not. If you're living at home, you might be in a situation where you must still attend your family's choice of religious services. Even if you hear anti-queer messages at these services, try not to take them to heart. These messages are often the result of fear and ignorance. Not everyone in your religion believes them and neither should you. Know that you are a good, kind person who is just as worthy as anyone else in your faith community.

**Q: I grew up dreaming about a wedding.
Do I have to give that up?**
A: During the last several years, same-sex marriage has been a topic of great debate. Unfortunately, what's considered legal and valid varies depending on where you live. Marriage or civil unions for same-sex couples have been legalized in Vermont, New Hampshire, Connecticut, Iowa, Massachusetts, and Washington, D.C. But in California, passage of the controversial Proposition 8 initiative for a time reversed the state's same-sex marriage law. And so, the debate continues.

But legal or not, many GLBTQ people still celebrate the special love and commitment between two people. They do this either by holding their own private ceremonies or by holding ceremonies within open and accepting religious communities. Same-sex weddings or commitment ceremonies don't mean that one person has to wear a tux and the other a dress, although you can definitely do that if you want. A ceremony can be however you and your partner want it. It can be a traditional wedding, take place on a beach, or be in your parents' backyard. It's up to you. If marriage is what you dreamed of, you don't have to give up that dream just because you're queer.

**Q: I'm fine with my religion.
What can I do to help others who are struggling?**
A: If you have been able to reconcile your religious or spiritual beliefs with your sexual orientation or gender identity, you have a

▼ Campaigning for Marriage Rights

Freedom to Marry (www.freedomtomarry.org). If you'd like to learn more about the debate over same-sex marriage in the United States or get involved in the fight for marriage rights, check out this group. The website includes facts about the issue, a blog, videos, and more. ▼

tremendous opportunity to help others. It doesn't matter whether it was easy for you or the result of intense soul searching. Many people have a tough time accepting themselves because of their religious backgrounds or beliefs. Sharing your experiences with them can provide the encouragement and help they might need on their own journeys.

You could become part of, or even form, an outreach group within your own congregation. Such groups offer those who are struggling an opportunity to talk with and hear from others who have had similar experiences. You could also look into working with an interfaith alliance that addresses issues related to GLBTQ people. These groups offer many opportunities to volunteer. Or you might join or start an Internet group for those who are struggling with religious issues.

Cultural Differences, Being GLBTQ, and You

Cultural traditions, like religious ones, could be a big part of your day-to-day life. Culture is composed of many things— race or ethnicity, religion, where you were born or raised, the language(s) you speak. Specifically, it might influence family traditions, holiday celebrations, how your family relates to one another, nicknames, what language you speak at home or with friends, the music you listen to, and the food you eat. Culture also can be a strong influence on gender and sex role expectations such as how you're supposed to behave, dress, and talk. It could even affect expectations for dating.

Reconciling your cultural and family traditions with the need to understand and accept your sexuality or gender identity can be a complex and sometimes painful process. You could feel like you're being forced to choose one identity or the other. For example, it might feel like you aren't allowed to be queer *and* a person of color. To make matters more complicated, GLBTQ people who belong to ethnic, racial, or social minorities are sometimes viewed as having "two strikes" (or more) against them in society. These individuals could face discrimination for being queer and for being African American, Latino, Asian, Pacific Islander, Arab, Native American, and so on.

Part of the struggle can be invisibility. You might feel like your culture doesn't have a place in it for openly GLBTQ people. Those who are queer are forced to keep a low profile. In many cultures, family and community are central parts of life. Your identity is influenced by how you relate to these groups and the roles you play within them. You might feel isolated or invisible in the queer community if you don't see others from similar backgrounds. Role models, community, and seeing yourself reflected in the society around you are important factors in being able to accept yourself.

No matter where you're from or what your ethnic background, there have been and are queer people in your culture. How they've been viewed and treated varies widely. Some GLBTQ people find that their racial or ethnic backgrounds make being queer, or at least being out, difficult for them.

For some, it's because many of their cultural traditions are tied to religious beliefs. For others, it's because being GLBTQ is seen as going against strongly held cultural beliefs about sex roles and gender expression. In some cultures, being queer is seen as undermining the family by not carrying on the family name or by going against family expectations. Coming out can be difficult in some cultures because it's seen as embarrassing or bringing shame on a family because it makes public something that is considered to be private.

These influences can form some powerful barriers to understanding and accepting GLBTQ people. Unfortunately, many queer people of color might feel isolated from their communities for these and other reasons.

▼ **For GLBTQ Teens of Color** There are many websites where queer people of color can socialize and connect on common issues. Some of the religion resources on pages 156–157 could also be helpful.

Ambiente Joven (www.ambientejoven.org). This Spanish-language site for queer Latino teens includes information on religion, sexuality, and safer sex, as well as resources throughout the United States and South America and links to other sites of interest.

AQU25A (www.apiwellness.org/youth.html). AQU25A, a program of the Asian & Pacific Islander Wellness Center, is for GLBTQ young adults ages 25 and under. Their site includes information and referrals, as well as information on activities in the San Francisco area.

Asian & Pacific Islander Family Pride (www.apifamilypride.org). Their mission is to foster acceptance of sexual and gender diversity among API families. The site includes links to API-specific resources, including books and videos.

Trikone (www.trikone.org). Trikone is a nonprofit organization for GLBTQ people of South Asian descent (including people from Afghanistan, Bangladesh, Bhutan, India, Maldives, Myanmar, Nepal, Pakistan, Sri Lanka, and Tibet). Its goals are to bring people of South Asian heritage together, help people affirm South Asian identity as well as their sexual orientation and gender identity, and fight discrimination.

Zuna Institute (www.zunainstitute.org). Zuna Institute explores issues related to being a black lesbian in today's society and advocates for civil rights. Their website includes information and resources, advocacy opportunities, and links to many other organizations and sites for black lesbians.

Many of the national organizations mentioned throughout this book include links and information specifically for queer teens of color. Additional groups for queer people of color are organized at the local level; a Web search could lead the way to local groups. ▼

BEEN THERE

"Being an African-American woman has made it more difficult to be GLBTQ. People make it an issue that I'm a lesbian and black — some say I won't succeed because of those factors combined. I know who I am. My culture and its negativity just make me stronger, because there is nothing worse than being ostracized by people you can identify with on many issues except this one. I've grown to not care how they feel about it because it doesn't matter how they feel, as long as I love myself." —Patrice, 20

"To address the issue of my heritage, I do identify with my Cherokee heritage. As does anything, it has shaped my character, but in small ways. My heritage and my sexuality were never at odds with each other." —Scott, 19

The traditions of other groups could have a very different impact on how you feel about yourself as a GLBTQ person in that culture. Some Native American cultures, for example, have a history of recognizing and accepting their GLBTQ members. Navajos have a word for people who are considered neither men nor women—*nadle*. The Lakota also have words to describe males and females who lived outside of typical gender roles—*winkte* and *koskalaka*. The Omahas have a word that means either someone who is neither male nor female, or for a transformation from a man or a woman to the opposite gender—*mexoga*. Certain societies don't just accept transgender people, but even look upon them with reverence.

More Cultural Factors

While religion and culture have a strong impact on personal identity, many other factors can affect how society sees you— and how you see yourself, both as an individual and as a queer person. Resolving identity issues can be difficult for GLBTQ people. It can be even more challenging for queer people who are seen as "different" in another way.

Anyone who does not fit with what society calls "norms" (but what are actually just averages) and who is also GLBTQ could be dealing with issues of identity, fitting in, and visibility on many levels. Just as there are norms in society, there are norms within the GLBTQ community that can lead you to have expectations about who's queer and what queerness supposedly looks like.

If your school has a GSA, think for a moment about all the different people who are members. You all could have a lot in common, but there are probably plenty of differences, too. And those differences, whether they're in the form of divergent interests, disabilities, economic background, or other things entirely, might leave you wondering where you fit in. They could leave you confronting the norms within society and also within the GLBTQ community.

For example, maybe you're in a wheelchair. Do you think people would be surprised to see you at a GSA meeting because they'd never thought about someone being disabled *and* queer before? You might face a similar reaction if you came out at a meeting of a disabled students group. This is just one example of what it can be like to try to figure out who you are and reconcile that with the many different communities of which you could be a part.

It can be a complicated process—one that will likely continue as you mature and experience different things. But diversity is a positive thing. It enriches our lives and the lives of those around us. If you think of yourself as a mosaic, and each aspect of who you are as one more colored tile, you'll see that each color contributes to creating the intricate and beautiful picture of who you are.

Being a Whole Person: Integrating All Parts of Yourself

If you're having a hard time reconciling your culture, religion, disability, and so on with being GLBTQ, you could be feeling alone, confused, or rejected. Figuring out where you fit in your culture as a queer person and how you can integrate your culture into your life can be a long process. It can help to remember that there are GLBTQ members of every race, religion, ethnicity, and cultural group. No matter who you are, you're not alone.

It might help to talk with other GLBTQ people with similar backgrounds, heritages, or experiences. If you're struggling with issues such as those related to race, ethnicity, and religion, talk to someone about it. Depending on where you live, support groups might be available. If not, the Internet can be a great place to touch base with people who understand what you're going through.

Chapter 10

Transgender Teens

**Sex is what's between your legs.
Gender is what's between your ears.**

BEEN THERE

"Since I was little I would always lay awake at night and wonder how much better my life would be if I had been born a girl. Then I would think, 'Oh great, the one thing I really want, I can't have.'"
—Alexandra, 14

In many ways, transgender (or trans) teens have a greater struggle for acceptance and understanding than other queer teens. Comparatively little is understood about being transgender, so trans teens can feel even more isolation and loneliness than their gay, lesbian, and bisexual peers. However, this is changing.

According to the Human Rights Campaign, knowledge of what the term *transgender* means, as well as familiarity with transgender public policy issues, is growing dramatically across the United States. This represents an important stride toward a tolerant society. More work definitely must be done to educate the public about the experiences of being a trans person, but acceptance *is* growing.

While more research about transgender teens has been done in recent years, it isn't known how many young people identify as trans. The lack of information about being trans has partly resulted from society's reluctance to acknowledge that being trans is a biological fact (not an emotional choice), and that being transgender is not an isolated experience. As with being gay, lesbian, or bisexual, some trans teens are told that they are just confused or are too young to be sure. Other teens are told that gender is a choice.

Unfortunately, many people still are ignorant of the feelings and experiences of trans people. Even in the medical community, it can be difficult for those who are transgender to find mental health professionals and physicians who are capable of providing educated, compassionate care.

But not everyone is in the dark about being trans. Counseling support and accurate information about being transgender *are* out there. If you're transgender or think you might be, it's important to reach out and seek help. Not because something is wrong with you, but because addressing trans issues is much easier if you have support and access to resources.

▼ **A Dance Evolution** Transgender people are becoming more visible and will continue to do so. The New York–based dance group Vogue Evolution made history by appearing on season four of MTV's *America's Best Dance Crew*. The openly gay crew, fronted by transgender woman Leiomy Maldonado, quickly became a fan favorite for their explosive dance moves and for their openness and confidence in expressing who they are. Throughout the season, viewers learned more about Leiomy, the first trans person to appear on the show, and some of her experiences as a young trans person. Since the show, the group has made appearances at a variety of events and has appeared on national television interviews. ▼

What Does It Mean to Be Transgender?

When you're transgender, you have a gender identity or expression that is different from your biological sex or physical anatomy. A few definitions might be helpful here. *Gender identity* is your internal sense of being male or female—basically what gender you consider yourself to be. Your *gender expression* is how you express your gender identity and includes the clothes you wear, your hairstyle, and your body language (how you walk, your posture, your gestures). In society, people often take their cues from someone's gender expression to assume that person's anatomical sex.

Transgender is a broad term that covers many different groups. It can include transsexuals (in all stages of transitioning), crossdressers, drag kings and queens, and people who are intersex, among many others (see the following Q&A for definitions of these terms). People who are trans might identify in a variety of ways. (For more about self-describing and its relevance, see page 174.)

What it feels like to be trans is different for every person, although many describe some common experiences, such as feeling "trapped in the wrong body." Others describe it more as having an internal sense of self that isn't reflected on the outside by their bodies. It can be confusing to feel female inside and look at yourself in the mirror and see an anatomical male looking back at you. Still others report that the experience of being a trans person can be incredibly liberating, freeing them from stereotypes and how gender is defined, expressed, and felt.

BEEN THERE

"From a very early age I knew I was different. I always preferred dressing up as a princess rather than a police officer or fireman. This carried on through my childhood and into my teenage years, when I became increasingly frustrated about not being able to be the girl I wanted to be. When I came out to my parents, I explained that I never felt right as a male, and that I always wanted to be a girl." —Alycia, 19

Trans Q&A

You might have a lot of questions about what it means to be transgender. If you do, you're not alone. While the GLBTQ community as a whole is working for greater visibility and more rights, gay, lesbian, and bisexual people still tend to receive more recognition and acceptance than those who are trans. As a result, it's still common for people to be uninformed about transgender issues. This sometimes is true even within the queer community.

Here are some common questions and answers about being transgender:

Q: Why are people transgender?
A: According to PFLAG, many in the scientific community believe that being transgender is the result of complicated biological factors that are determined by the time someone is born. This means that you don't become transgender or choose to be transgender—you're born a trans person.

Q: Is being transgender a mental disorder?
A: The mental health community labels one aspect of the transgender experience as *gender dysphoria*—a term for the pain, anxiety, and confusion that can result when a person's gender identity and biological sex don't match. The pressure to conform to accepted gender roles/expression and a general lack of acceptance from society also can contribute to gender dysphoria.

Mental health professionals often diagnose transgender people with *gender identity disorder (GID)*. Transgender activist and health researcher Jessica Xavier explains that some trans people struggle with the advantages and disadvantages of being diagnosed with GID. A diagnosis

The Debate Over GID

The classification of transgenderism as a disorder remains the subject of much debate. In fact, homosexuality was classified as a disorder in the *Diagnostic and Statistical Manual of Mental Disorders (DSM)* until 1974. It's possible that the classification regarding transgenderism will change, as well. In 2013, the American Psychiatric Association will publish a new edition of the DSM. The proposed revisions to the new edition include revised gender-related diagnoses, including a new diagnosis called *gender incongruence.*

of GID enables access to mental and physical treatment, which can be especially helpful for people trying to physically transition their genders. The downside of a GID diagnosis can be the stigma of being diagnosed with a mental disorder, which might encourage people to treat trans people like they're sick or mentally ill.

It's important to note that although the GID classification is labeled as a disorder, it doesn't mean that trans people are mentally ill. Treatment for GID generally (though not always) involves physical modifications to help bring one's body into harmony with one's emotional and mental self—not vice versa.

Q: Do all trans people want to have surgery to change their anatomies?

A: No. Many people do, but others do not. According to the Gay and Lesbian Medical Association, roughly 1,600–2,000 people undergo gender reassignment surgery in the United States each year.

In an effort to deal with their gender dysphoria, many trans people do go through a period of *gender transition*. During this time, they begin to change their appearance, and often their body, to match their gender identity. This might mean that they start wearing different clothing and changing their hairstyles to reflect the gender they feel they are on the inside. People may also change how they walk or move and adjust the sound of their voices. Some undergo minor cosmetic procedures such as electrolysis (permanent body hair removal) as well.

Gender transition doesn't necessarily mean surgery. It is a misconception that all trans people want to change their anatomies through *sex reassignment surgery (SRS)*. Sex reassignment surgery modifies primary sex characteristics (the genitals) and is sometimes accompanied by surgeries on secondary sex characteristics as well (such as breasts or the Adam's apple). People who don't identify with the sex they were born as, and who might change their bodies through hormones and surgery to reconcile their gender identity and physical sex, are referred to as *transsexual*. All transsexual people are considered transgender, but not all transgender people are transsexual.

Nonoperative transsexuals might not be interested in or able to have surgery (which can be very expensive). They may or may not take hormones as part of the transition process. Some

▼ A Victory for Trans People On February 2, 2010, the U.S. Tax Court ruled that Rhiannon O'Donnabhain, a postoperative trans woman, should be allowed to deduct the cost of her sex-change operation (about $25,000). O'Donnabhain had deducted the expenses when filing her taxes, but the IRS rejected the deduction on the grounds that the surgery was not medically necessary. In its decision, the U.S. Tax Court stated that the IRS's position was, "at best a superficial characterization of the circumstances" that is "thoroughly rebutted by the medical evidence." The legal group Gay & Lesbian Advocates & Defenders represented O'Donnabhain. ▼

trans people take hormones and go no further in physically transitioning. Others are preoperative transsexuals—they might be in the process of transition and plan to have sex reassignment surgery. Other trans people are postoperative transsexuals, which means they have had the hormone therapies and surgeries needed to complete a physical transition. Surgery is usually restricted to those over the age of 18, although this matter is the topic of much debate.

Q: What does *intersex* mean?
A: Intersex people are born with both male and female genitals, or with ambiguous genitalia. Some intersex people have surgeries, often in infancy and throughout childhood, to definitively assign them one anatomical sex. The surgery doesn't always result in a physical sex assignment that matches the person's internal gender. As a result, some intersex people grow up with gender identity issues that mirror those experienced by trans-gender people.

Q: Who are crossdressers?
A: Crossdressers (once called transvestites) are people who dress in clothing traditionally worn by the opposite sex. They might do this in private or in public. Crossdressers can be male or female, and they may be straight, gay, lesbian, or bisexual. Crossdressing does not necessarily indicate that a person is trans.

Q: Are transgender people also gay, lesbian, or bisexual?
A: Some are, but many are not. It's a common misconception that transgender people are all gay, lesbian, or bisexual. In fact, many trans people are straight. Some trans people are assumed to be lesbian or gay because of their gender expression.

However, some straight trans people might at first come out as gay, lesbian, or bisexual. Even though they have a different gender identity, they're attracted to persons of the same anatomical sex, but they haven't explored the possibility of being transgender. Other people who eventually realize they are transgender may initially perceive feelings of being of the opposite anatomical sex to mean that they're gay or lesbian. This is probably because gay and lesbian people are generally more visible in society than transgender people. It might not be clear to a teen that he is transgender because he doesn't know (or know about) transgender people or just hasn't reached that point yet in his identity formation.

BEEN THERE
"I spent a period of my life going out with other girls, as lesbians. But something didn't quite feel right. I've always wanted to be a guy, physically." —Kevin, 18

Q: If many transgender people are straight, why are they often lumped together with gay, lesbian, and bisexual people?
A: Transgender people share much of the same struggle for acceptance, recognition, and civil rights as gay, lesbian, and bisexual people. The issues of gender expression and sexual orientation often overlap. Frequently anti-queer bias and behavior have a lot to do with gender expression (rather than sexual orientation).

A female who wears her hair short and prefers to wear traditionally male clothing might be harassed or called a lesbian because she's stepping outside her traditional gender role. She might be lesbian or bisexual, she might be transgender, or she could just like having short hair and wearing more traditionally masculine clothing. People aren't reacting to her sexual orientation, they're responding to her gender expression. Some people feel threatened or afraid and might discriminate or get angry when they see people expressing their gender in nontraditional ways. Gay, lesbian, bisexual, and trans people often face this same discrimination when they don't conform to other people's ideas of gender. It's also possible for straight people to face this form of discrimination.

Transgender people have at times even faced discrimination from the gay, lesbian, and bisexual communities. This has been due to a lack of understanding about trans issues and an unwillingness to work together for greater acceptance of all GLBTQ people. One of the great things about GLBTQ teens today is their increased willingness to be inclusive and not draw lines between what it means to be gay, lesbian, bisexual, or transgender.

Describing Your Gender Identity

Because transgender is a blanket term that covers several distinct but related groups of people, self-description can be important to many trans people. People who are transgender may use a variety of different terms to describe themselves (self-identify).

There is some debate in the trans community about what terms can be applied to who. For example, some postoperative transsexuals—those who have taken hormones and had surgeries to more accurately reflect their gender identities—don't call themselves transsexuals. As far as they're concerned, they have become members of the opposite sex.

In the end, how a person identifies is a very personal decision. No one but the individual can choose what label to use. People choose to identify in many different ways: transgender, female-to-male (FTM), male-to-female (MTF), genderqueer, gender neutral, multi-gender, transman, boi, and

Two-Spirit People

Many Native American tribes have special words, and even hold reverence, for people who today would be characterized as transgender. Certain Native American cultures described transgender people as having "two spirits." Generally, Two-Spirit people are born one sex, but take on the gender roles for both sexes (though this definition varies somewhat across cultures). Two-Spirit people were often revered as healers, peacemakers, and shamans. Today, some trans people still identify as Two Spirit.

many others. How you identify (if you choose to at all) should be, first and foremost, comfortable and meaningful for you.

How Do You Know?
Figuring Out If You're Transgender

As with figuring out if you're gay, lesbian, or bisexual, self-discovery is a process. Maybe you've felt like someone of the opposite sex for as long as you can remember. Or perhaps you've only had a vague feeling of being different that you haven't been able to define. You might arrive at the conclusion that you're transgender relatively easily, or it could take months or years to figure out.

There isn't a checklist that can clearly indicate if you're transgender, but trans people do tend to share some common experiences. Perhaps some of these are familiar to you:

Have you ever felt like there is a conflict between your body and your mind? People often describe the experience of being transgender as feeling like they're trapped in the wrong body. Today's teens, though, because of increased openness toward exploring a variety of gender roles and ways of expressing gender identity, sometimes describe being transgender as feeling gender neutral, gender different, or simply "other." Some trans teens feel confusion over issues of gender while others are comfortable mentally and emotionally residing in that more fluid gray area of gender identity.

As you grow up, especially as you go through puberty, it's common to have some feelings of gender confusion, or of openness to gender exploration and fluidity of gender expression. That doesn't necessarily mean that you're trans, or even gay, lesbian, or bisexual. Part of being a teen is evolving into a stronger sense of yourself. For many, that evolution continues for years, possibly an entire lifetime. And as long as you understand that whoever you are is okay at any stage of your life, that's a good thing.

Do you dislike or avoid activities and interests that are usually associated with people of your birth sex? Dr. Milton Diamond writes that many trans people describe disliking and avoiding activities that are traditionally associated with people of their anatomical sex. Instead, they strongly prefer activities and behaviors that are traditionally linked with the sex with which they identify more. Often these likes, dislikes, and ways of behaving are obvious from an early age. For example, a young boy might enjoy playing with girls rather than roughhousing with other boys. He might hate sports, avoiding them in favor of playing dress-up and experimenting with his mother's makeup.

It's important to remember that being uncomfortable with or failing to embrace traditional gender roles doesn't necessarily mean someone is transgender. Many young people who are not transgender engage in a variety of activities and behaviors that

You GO Girls
Challenging Gender Roles in History: In early 18th-century Germany, a woman named Catharina Margaretha Linck dressed as a man, served in the army, and then went to work as a cotton dyer. Catharina even married a woman (although the bond technically wouldn't have been legal). During the Revolutionary War, Deborah Sampson dressed as a man and joined the Continental Army. Deborah was also known to have had romantic relationships with other women.

aren't necessarily associated with their biological sex. In the case of most transgender people, however, it goes beyond exploring. They have very strong, almost overpowering feelings related to their interests and behaviors.

Do you have thoughts of wanting to be the opposite physical sex? It's one thing to occasionally have a thought like, "Life would be easier if I were a guy," or, "I wonder what it would be like to be a girl?" It's another to have a persistent desire to actually be the opposite sex.

BEEN THERE

"I've always been fascinated with the idea of being a girl, I guess. I used to watch this show about a boy who suddenly acquires the ability to become a girl when he comes into contact with hot water. I could never really understand, though, why he was so very distressed about being a girl." —Chris, 19

Do you identify strongly with experiences of people who are transgender? One way to explore your gender identity is to find out more about trans people. It can be helpful to read about their experiences or talk with someone who identifies as transgender. You could find that, while people use different language to describe their experiences and feelings, what they're talking about really resonates with you and is something you can identify with.

▼ **Dirt Diva** Professional mountain bike racer Michelle Dumaresq is a postoperative trans woman. Dumaresq entered her sport in 2001, six years after completing SRS. She appeared in *Dirt Divas,* a film about female mountain bikers, and is the subject and star of the documentary *100% Woman.* Dumaresq's participation in female competitions has not been without controversy, as some believe she has an unfair advantage because she was born male. Dumaresq has commented, "I never set out to change the world or anything, I just want to race a bike." ▼

Now What? Options for Trans Teens

What do you do when you realize you're transgender? This is a complex question, and it's one that has many possible answers. You could wait and think about things. You could come out as transgender. You could decide to change your name or start dressing differently and possibly start transitioning socially into your gender identity. Or you could decide that you need your body to reflect your identity and start looking into procedures for physically transitioning.

But the first thing you'll need to do is accept yourself. Try to resist any urges you might have to label yourself as odd or abnormal. This can be very difficult for some people. Being a trans person doesn't mean something is wrong with you. It's part of who you are and there is nothing wrong with that. It might take time to come to terms with being transgender, and you might need help to work through what being trans means for your future.

Read All About It
Gender Spectrum (www.genderspectrum.org). This website provides practical information to help teens and their families understand the concepts of gender identity and expression. It includes a wealth of resources, Web links, and other media (including materials in Spanish).

Coping with Negative Emotions

Even if you've realized and accepted that you are transgender, your process probably isn't over. According to PFLAG, unlike gay, lesbian, and bisexual people who feel conflicted largely as a result of an emotional dilemma, trans people feel conflicted because of a physical dilemma. A disparity between gender identity and physical self can create an ongoing struggle.

That continuing struggle can have devastating emotional effects, particularly if the trans person believes there's no hope for change or progress. According to a study published in the *Journal of Homosexuality,* 33 percent of trans teens have attempted suicide. That's *one-third.*

Because you're working through emotional and identity issues that can be very complicated, it's important to get help. Here are some ways to do that.

Find support. You might reach out to family members, friends, adults at school, or others you trust. It's important to find support from those who are nonjudgmental. The people you talk to should listen to you and your feelings with your best interests in mind, not push their own agenda onto you. Talk with those who will take time with you and who won't discount your feelings as "a phase." Even if you have family and friend support, it's a good idea to talk with a trained professional at some point, preferably someone knowledgeable in transgender issues. Being transgender can evoke a lot of complex feelings, and it's helpful to talk to someone who understands that.

If you don't feel comfortable talking with someone you know, don't give up. A lot of resources are available to you. In addition to national organizations, many local groups support trans people. A variety of websites have bulletin boards, forums, or chats where you can communicate with other trans people. See page 180 for a list of resources.

Seek counseling. Researcher and transgender activist Jessica Xavier advises trans people to seek counseling, not because something is wrong with them that needs to be changed, but

▼ **Camp Aranu'tiq** Ever wish you could be around others who understand what it's like to be trans? Camp Aranu'tiq is a weeklong, tuition-free overnight summer camp held in Southern New England for transgender and gender variant young people ages 8–15. *Aranu'tiq* is a Chugach (an indigenous people of Alaska) word for a person thought to embody both the male and female spirit. Such people were revered because of their ability to transcend traditional gender norms. For more information, visit www.camparanutiq.org. ▼

because it's a way to get needed support. Therapy should be aimed at helping you understand, accept, and feel good about your personal identity. (If your counselor tries to convince you to deny your gender identity or conform, seek out someone else.) It's common for people to feel uncomfortable about gender issues and internalize fears about trans people. A skilled counselor can address these issues and help you understand that absolutely nothing is wrong with who you are. You might start your search for a counselor by contacting a local or national GLBTQ or trans organization.

Coming Out

After you realize you're trans, you might decide to come out. It could be to only a few close friends or family members, or it could be to many people. This is particularly important if you want to start living in a way that better reflects your gender identity. Transgender people who wish to transition their genders are usually forced to come out because changes are so obvious to others.

▼ Organizations for Transgender People

ACT for Youth (www.actforyouth.net). ACT for Youth was created as a resource for those who work with transgender teens. It includes an outstanding assortment of resources including publications and links for teens, parents, educators, and others.

International Foundation for Gender Education (IFGE) (www.ifge .org). This group is an advocacy and educational organization that promotes acceptance of trans people. It maintains a bookstore and publishes a magazine on transgender issues. The website provides a wide variety of links and information.

TransFamily (www.transfamily.org). TransFamily provides support, education, advocacy, and outreach for the trans community and their families and friends. The organization offers information and operates an emergency resource hotline at (216) 691-4357.

Human Rights Campaign (www.hrc.org). Human Rights Campaign offers the latest information on advocacy for transgender people. Visit their site for the latest on legislative issues. ▼

Coming out—whatever the circumstances—can be a stressful process for everyone involved. And just like coming out as gay, lesbian, or bisexual, the people you're coming out to might react in many different ways. Some may be accepting, others might be confused, sad, or angry. (See Chapter 3 for advice on coming out.) The people you're coming out to also might be confused if you've previously come out to them as gay, lesbian, or bisexual.

According to Jessica Xavier and PFLAG, parents especially might have serious difficulties dealing with their children coming out as transgender. Some believe they're losing a son or daughter. When a teen tells family adults that she wants to live her life as someone of a different gender, they might experience feelings of grief similar to death. It might feel like the daughter they raised has suddenly been taken from them.

The people you come out to might not understand what it means to be transgender and may have a lot of questions for you. It can be hard for your parents and other people who care about you to learn that you have been struggling with such difficult issues. They might worry about you and your future. However, they might want to help and support you.

BEEN THERE

"Coming out trans was the most nerve racking thing I have ever done. I had my doubts, but I had made up my mind it had to be done. My parents were shocked, as I expected, but they seemed to be happy that I'd told them. We talked about the possibilities for me for hours. They said as long as I'm happy, they'd support me in whatever I wanted to do." —Alycia, 19

"My dad discovered I was trans when he saw some sites I'd been looking at online. He eventually just said, 'So, let's talk about what you look at on the Internet.' This was my cue to explain to him everything. He asked a lot of questions. He was very curious about me. He had done an amazing amount of research on the Internet himself. He looked up sex reassignment surgery doctors, including how much the procedure would cost. He found out all he could on hormones, and he even contacted a male-to-female trans person for information that might help me out. It did. It helped me out immensely just to know that there is someone who cares about me." —Amanda, 18

When you come out, it's important to let your family and loved ones know that resources are available to help them, too. (See page 180 for a list of transgender resources.) Many national transgender organizations will help you find local support via websites or phone referrals. Your local phone directory might list additional resources. PFLAG also offers services for trans people and their families and friends, including an excellent brochure titled "Welcoming Our Trans Family and Friends."

Changing Names

One of the first things many transgender people do is change their names to better reflect their gender identities. As a teen, you can't legally change your name without a parent's consent. But some teens do change their names in practice, asking families and friends to use their preferred names.

Changing your name to one that reflects who you are can be a positive way to assert your true identity. It can sometimes be difficult to get people to take your name change seriously or to accept it. Some parents, friends, and school administrators will be very supportive and accepting. Others will reject the idea completely.

If you're certain that you are transgender and you're thinking about changing your name, here are some things to consider:

Come out first. Telling your family and friends that you're transgender and, in the same breath, asking them to call you by a different name can be a lot for people to process. It's likely that they'll have a lot of questions about what it means to be transgender. If you can help them understand that, they may be in a better place to understand why you want to change your name. However, if your parents seem fairly receptive to your coming out, you might want to discuss your name of choice right away. It's up to you, but take it one step at a time and allow your family and friends to do the same.

Try to be patient. Some people will be respectful of your request to use your new name. Others will not. Even those who are respectful will probably need time to get used to the change.

According to clinical psychologist Dr. Sandy Loiterstein, a name change can be very difficult for parents to accept. They may see it as a rejection of something very personal they have given a son or daughter. Changing names can also deepen the grieving process many parents of transgender people go through because it can emphasize the idea of loss.

If your parents are struggling, it can be helpful for you together to see a therapist knowledgeable about transgender issues. Counseling can help them understand what you're facing and help them adjust to your transgender identity.

Choose your name carefully. Put some thought into your new name. Choose one that's representative of your personality or meaningful for you in some way. Also, it's usually a good idea to choose a somewhat conventional name. If you ask people to call you something outrageous, chances are they won't take you seriously.

Some trans people choose names that are feminine or masculine versions of their birth names. So Sam becomes Samantha and Charlotte becomes Charles. Others choose gender-neutral names, such as Alex or Chris. Some people might choose another name entirely. The most important thing is that you pick a name that feels like you.

If you want to change the name you use at school, get your parents' support. It can be extremely difficult to get teachers and staff to use your new name at school. But having your parents behind you can help. They can be sources of support as you're talking with your principal, school counselor, or teachers. Sometimes changing your name at school is easier if you're starting classes in a different building or a new grade. People might have less to associate with your previous name.

Some transgender teens choose to use their birth names at school (or have to if their school refuses to use their new names) and use their chosen names at other times, depending on who they're with and where they are. And some trans teens decide to wait until they're older to change their names, either legally or in everyday life.

Gender Transitioning

For some people, a change in name is the first step in gender transitioning. Gender transitioning is a complex, multi-step process of starting to live full time as a person of a different gender. Transitioning doesn't, by definition, include surgery or other physical changes, though for some people it does. It primarily involves factors that affect how you relate to others and how they relate to you. It might include changing your name, dressing differently, and altering other aspects of your appearance (like hair or makeup). It can also mean changing your mannerisms, voice, and how you move.

Gender transitioning can also involve many physical changes for some trans people. A physical transition might include taking hormones or other substances under the supervision of a medical professional. For some, transitioning may also include surgery. This is an option almost always reserved for adults. As a transgender teen it is very unlikely that you can undergo sex reassignment surgery, although you might be able to work with an endocrinologist who can assist you with hormone treatments. It is rare to find physicians willing to prescribe hormones to those under 18, but some will.

BEEN THERE

"Perhaps it all began when I was but a child, maybe six years old, watching Saturday morning cartoons — specifically, Bugs Bunny donning a dress and wig. I was enthralled at the transformation. This, I decided, was what I would aspire to. That's as far back as I can recall about my 'difference.'" — Zelia, 15

Physical Transitioning

Undergoing a physical gender transition can be a long and complex process. For some transgender people who wish to undergo a full physical change, it can be a vital and rewarding process. Many steps and medical professionals are involved, and some services can be very difficult for those under 18 to obtain. It is extremely rare that minors are allowed to undergo full physical transitions. Sex reassignment surgeries also are very expensive, and many people save for a long time to afford them.

The physical transitioning process takes a long time for many reasons. Some physical changes take months or even a few years to complete. Medical professionals must supervise the physical transitioning process, and they can help you explore feelings and decisions along the way.

If you want to transition, especially if you want to pursue sex reassignment surgery (SRS), you'll need to know about the Standards of Care. These guidelines were created by the World Professional Association for Transgender Health (formerly the Harry Benjamin International Gender Dysphoria Association). They are the standards under which most trans people obtain hormone therapy and SRS. Few surgeons perform SRS, but most, if not all of them, follow these standards.

The Standards of Care include a period of psychotherapy (to confirm someone is a trans person), the beginning of hormone therapy (which is a lifelong process), the administration of the Real-Life Experience (living full time as your intended gender for a period of time), and finally, if desired, SRS.

Typically, a period of psychotherapy is required *before* a person begins taking hormones. The therapy and assessment period can last for three months or longer, depending on the mental health professional and the person receiving treatment. Young people often feel like the validity of their transgender identity is being questioned. It might seem like the professionals assessing them believe they're going through a phase or overreacting. It can be frustrating to feel like others are second-guessing something you're very certain about. Try to release those feelings in a positive way, like by writing about them in a journal. (See Chapter 8, beginning on page 129, for more ideas for dealing with negative feelings.)

BEEN THERE

"I think the most difficult part of being transgender is the way my gender identity and my body just don't match. It's a constant source of frustration and annoyance for me. I'm not currently on hormones because I have not had enough counseling yet. One of the things that annoys me most is others having the attitude that they have to protect a young transsexual from herself." —Rylan, 19

The Real-Life Experience is a period (a minimum of one year) during which a transitioning person must live and work, if he is in the work world, full time as someone of the sex that matches his gender identity. In other words, a female-to-male (FTM) person would have to live as a man for a minimum of one year. This isn't a traditional test, as you might think of one. It's more of an experience monitored by medical professionals. According to the Standards of Care guidelines, the purpose of the experience is "to allow you to overcome awkwardness, establish new behavior patterns, and approach unfamiliar situations with an unforced inner confidence."

Only after successful completion of the Real-Life Experience (as determined by a supervising physician) can a person become a candidate for SRS. "Success" in this case is not an indicator that the person has done something correctly, but that the experience has confirmed that the person truly wants and can handle the physical transition.

Sex reassignment surgery involves the permanent refashioning of the sexual anatomy. Beyond genital surgery, many trans people undergo additional procedures. Male-to-female trans might have facial and body hair removed, an operation to reduce the size of the Adam's apple, and various cosmetic surgeries to achieve a more feminine-looking face and body. Some might also have breast augmentation surgery, though many just rely on their hormone treatments (which cause the body to develop breasts) and/or surgery on their genitalia. Female-to-male trans might have their breasts removed and/or surgery on their genitalia. Even with these procedures, being able to "pass" as your new physical sex isn't guaranteed. Some people never pass completely. But many do.

Some teens get impatient with the transitioning process or find it difficult to obtain hormones from a doctor or clinic, so they buy hormones on the street. This could have serious negative physical and legal consequences. As with other drugs, hormones bought on the street could contain anything and their

A Note on Passing

"Passing" refers to being able to appear or live as your opposite physical sex without being noticed as a transgender person. This term is controversial because some think the concept of passing is offensive—it implies that people who cannot pass 100 percent of the time are somehow less than those who can. But does it matter if someone can tell or suspects that you're trans? Some people believe that it shouldn't matter. How you feel about it is up to you.

strength and dosage is unknown. Hormones should be taken only under the supervision of a doctor, preferably an endocrinologist, and at the proper dosage (which varies from person to person). If you're under 18, you might have to wait a while to obtain hormones legally.

Trans Pride: Responding to Transphobia

Transphobia is still common because traditional ideas about gender and gender roles tend to be so deeply rooted in society. The general lack of understanding about what it means to be trans can make it difficult for transgender people to find acceptance from their families, school officials, and society as a whole. Transphobia can lead to name-calling and discrimination and can also escalate into harassment and even violence.

As with homophobia, you can respond to transphobia in many different ways—by ignoring it, speaking up, attempting to educate people, or getting involved in working for change. However, be very careful to assess the situation before deciding how to respond. According to GLSEN, trans students and others who challenge traditional gender roles in obvious ways often endure the greatest harassment and worst physical attacks. While safety is a big concern for gay, lesbian, and bisexual students, it is a huge concern for many transgender students.

If you're being harassed at school and adults there refuse to act, you can get help. Organizations such as GLSEN, the National Gay and Lesbian Task Force (NGLTF), and the American Civil Liberties Union (ACLU) can help you fight discrimination in your school. Transgender and gender rights advocacy groups can help, too. Contact information for these groups can be found on page 180 or in the Resources section, beginning on page 207.

Facing Discrimination

Social pressures to conform to gender stereotypes can be extreme. Because gender expression is so visible and obvious, it's easy to find yourself facing unwanted attention or harassment. Trans people who are transitioning, or those who can't pass, can be especially vulnerable to harassment and physical abuse. While there are currently few legal protections for trans people, the climate is starting to change. For example, there is a push to add transgender people to protections that include sex and sexual orientation. The Matthew Shepard and James Byrd Jr. Hate Crimes Prevention Act, passed in 2009, covers crimes motivated by a victim's actual or perceived gender, sexual orientation, gender identity, or disability. For information on the most current legislation, visit the HRC website (www.hrc.org).

Just as with gay, lesbian, and bisexual people, discrimination against and abuse of trans people is *never* okay and it is *never* justifiable. If you have been attacked, report the attack to the police. If the police refuse to recognize your claim or file a report, a national organization such as Lambda Legal (www.lambdalegal.org), the National Gay and Lesbian Task Force (www.ngltf.org), or the ACLU (www.aclu.org) might be able to help. Many transgender groups can also help (see page 180). These organizations advocate for trans people and lobby for their legal rights. You do not have to suffer alone or in silence.

Trans people also can face discrimination at work, in part because the transition process is so readily apparent. In 2009, transgender activists succeeded in getting an amendment added to the Employment Non-Discrimination Act (ENDA). If passed, this act would make discrimination in the workplace based on sexual orientation or gender identity illegal. (For more on ENDA, see page 193.)

In spite of the harsh discrimination many trans people face, increasing numbers of people are coming out as transgender. This increased visibility will help educate others about what it means to be trans. Transgender people can face difficult issues, but many live very meaningful, fulfilled, and happy lives. The most important thing you can do is accept yourself for the wonderful person you are.

Chapter 11

Work, College, and Beyond

Life, liberty, and the pursuit of happiness are not "special rights."

Many teens enter the work world during high school. For others, college comes first and work and careers are something they plan to address afterward. Either way, if you're GLBTQ, entering the workforce or choosing a college can present questions straight peers don't have to consider.

Finding a GLBTQ-Friendly Company

Some teens don't care if an employer is GLBTQ-friendly. For others, it's a very important part. Regardless of how you feel, it's helpful to know where you stand. Increasingly, public and private employers are including sexual orientation in their nondiscrimination policies. Unfortunately, far fewer include gender identity (although this is changing).

Employers tend to be open with prospective and current employees about their human resources policies. You should be able to find out fairly easily whether a nondiscrimination policy is in place. You can search a company's website or ask one of its representatives. An employee handbook should also contain information about the company's nondiscrimination policy. Many companies post their policies in lunch or breakrooms, print them on job applications, or hand out copies automatically with any other employment-related paperwork.

The Human Rights Campaign (HRC) is another source of information for GLBTQ issues on the job. The group regularly updates a Corporate Equality Index, which rates employers based on GLBTQ friendliness. HRC also maintains a database of employers that lets you search for companies that include GLBTQ people in their nondiscrimination policies, offer domestic partner/same-sex spouse benefits, or have queer employee groups. Visit HRC's website (www.hrc.org) to access these features.

According to HRC, 305 of the 590 businesses it surveyed in 2009 achieved top ratings for being GLBTQ-friendly. This is up from 260 businesses just one year prior—a significant gain. These 305 companies collectively employ more than 9 million full-time employees. Workers at these companies are protected from employment discrimination based on sexual orientation and gender identity/expression by employers' policies in areas such as diversity, training, and benefits.

Transgender workers have made major gains since the Corporate Equality Index was first published. In 2002, just 5 percent of rated businesses prohibited discrimination based on gender identity or expression. In 2010, that figure had increased dramatically to 72 percent.

Being GLBTQ in the Workplace: Your Decisions and Your Rights

People approach being GLBTQ in the workplace in many different ways. Some prefer to remain private about being queer, not addressing it unless it happens to come up. Others feel it's important to have coworkers know they are queer. There's no right or wrong way to address this issue. Do what you feel comfortable doing for the specific situation you are in.

Should I Tell a Prospective Employer I'm GLBTQ?

Often queer people wonder whether they should come out to a potential employer during an interview. That's really a personal decision. Especially for teens, many believe that telling others they're GLBTQ should be on a "need to know" basis. If it somehow relates to the job (like applying for a position at a GLBTQ organization), then it could be appropriate to share.

Some people who are completely out prefer to be open about who they are from the beginning to make sure their gender identity or sexual orientation won't be a problem in the workplace. But telling an employer that you're GLBTQ during an interview can create an uncomfortable situation for you both. Whether you're GLBTQ or straight doesn't have anything to do with how well you can do your job, but coming out in an interview might give that impression. The focus is really on finding out whether the job is a good match for you. You can also try to figure out whether the company is GLBTQ-friendly, but you don't have to come out to do that.

Here are questions you can ask to determine whether a company is queer-friendly:

Ask about the company's policies. "Do you have an employment nondiscrimination policy? Who does it cover?" or "Does your employment nondiscrimination policy cover GLBTQ people?" If you're concerned about expressing that level of detail, you could just ask to see a copy of the policy.

Ask, "How is this workplace environment for GLBTQ employees?" This gives an obvious indication that you're GLBTQ, so it's up to you to decide if you're comfortable with that.

Some transgender people choose to come out during an interview, especially if they dress as the opposite anatomical sex. Unfortunately, some degree of workplace discrimination against trans people is not uncommon. (The companies that scored 100 percent in HRC's Corporate Equality Index all include gender identity in their nondiscrimination policies.)

Should I Come Out to My Coworkers?

Coming out to coworkers can be a great experience because it can result in a more open and supportive work environment, one where you feel free to be yourself. But remember, people you work with don't have to be your best friends. It's up to you how much personal information you want them to know.

As you spend more time in the working world, you'll come across people whose religious, political, and social beliefs are very different from yours, and not necessarily in a good way. Sometimes these encounters can be stressful or annoying. But, for some of the people you're exposed to, you might be the first person they know to be queer. You could have a positive influence on their beliefs.

For those who prefer not to come out as GLBTQ at work, that's okay. It's important to do what you're comfortable with. And that could change over time.

What Are My Rights?

Currently, no federal antidiscrimination law fully protecting GLBTQ people from job discrimination exists, so queer rights in the workplace vary by employer and geographic location. Some states—but not all—have enacted laws that cover job discrimination. At least for now, your rights depend largely on where you live or work.

BEEN THERE

"I think that the quality of life for GLBTQ people in this country is getting better, but it certainly isn't great. There are a lot of benefits and rights that GLBTQ people are not allowed to receive. Being gay didn't really affect me negatively until I started to witness the hatred and bigotry in this world. But once I started to get out and see that other gay people have made it through, I started to feel much better about being a gay person in this country." —Bengie, 15

More progressive companies have added phrases like "sexual orientation" and "gender identity" to their nondiscrimination policies, so while their home states might not have protections in place for queer people, the company does.

Civil rights and GLBTQ activists are currently lobbying hard to get the Employment Non-Discrimination Act (ENDA) passed. If passed, ENDA would be a federal law that provides basic protections against discrimination in the workplace based on sexual orientation, as well as gender identity or expression. It would be illegal to fire, deny employment, or harass someone because of his or her actual or perceived sexual orientation or gender identity. Many major corporations have endorsed the bill.

I Am Being Discriminated Against in My Workplace, What Should I Do?

Discrimination can take many forms. Sexual harassment, off-color remarks, and passing up someone for a promotion because he is GLBTQ are all forms of discrimination. Queer people do sometimes face workplace discrimination, but you should neither expect it nor accept it.

Here are some tips for what to do if you think you are being discriminated against by an employer:

1. Stop and think. Think carefully about the situation. Are you sure you're being discriminated against because you're GLBTQ? You might be. It's also possible that you're misreading the situation. Stop and assess it. Does your employer have a history of anti-GLBTQ behavior? Could you have misunderstood something that was said? If you have a trusted coworker, ask for her advice. Tell her what was said to you or what you overheard and ask for her opinion. The human resources department should also be able to help (though discrimination could also come from HR).

2. Write it down. If you suspect (or know) you're being discriminated against because you're GLBTQ, write down the incident and include names of anyone else who might have witnessed it. If several incidents occur, keep track of all of them. Keep a record of any interactions you have with your employer regarding the matter and include her responses. This record will be very useful if the issue is not resolved and you decide to take further action. Most human resources representatives will tell you that documenting these incidents is the first step in enabling them to investigate.

3. Come up with a plan. If you have a human resources representative helping you, he will help you formulate a plan or, more likely, will have a pre-determined set of actions to follow. These generally follow legal regulations and guidelines.

If you're handling it on your own because you don't have access to human resources help, plan what you will say to your employer or coworker and approach her calmly and rationally. Ask to speak with her and then sit down and explain the situation and why you feel you were discriminated against.

Then—and this step is critical—listen to her response. She might offer an explanation that puts your concerns to rest, so give her that opportunity. She might confess to the discrimination or she might deny it completely. Regardless of her response, try to stay calm. You're more likely to be taken seriously if you can remain professional.

4. If her response is negative, decide your course of action. You have several options. You can go back to work and ignore it, you can quit your job, or you can try to address the issue in another way. There isn't one right way to deal with the situation, just what's right for you. You might not have the time, energy, or money (in the case of a legal response) to address the issue. You might really need the job. Or you might feel like the situation is one you just can't live with.

If your issue is with a coworker or direct supervisor, it might be time to go to his boss. Again, remember step three—stay calm and rational. Keep your comments to facts and not opinions.

If you decide to pursue the matter, HRC and Lambda Legal are two groups that can counsel you about your rights according to your state's laws. They also can refer you to lawyers in your area, if necessary.

Discrimination can be demeaning and frustrating. Regardless of how you decide to deal with it, be sure to remind yourself that discrimination is a result of ignorance. It has nothing to do with you as a person.

A Perfect Match: Finding the Right School

If you're going to college, picking the right one (or technical or vocational school) can be challenging. First you have to go through what every other college-bound teen goes through: deciding on a state school or a private college; choosing a liberal arts program or something more specialized; figuring out what you can afford; applying for scholarships or financial aid. But once you've narrowed it down, how can you be sure you'll be going into an environment that's supportive of GLBTQ people?

Tips for Finding a GLBTQ-Friendly College

If you're interested in finding a GLBTQ-friendly college, it's not as hard as you might think. Here are some ideas that can help.

Search the Internet. Using a search engine, look for schools using terms like "gay-friendly colleges." Many queer websites and publications have articles about queer-friendly colleges. Some even poll their readers to find out what's what.

You also can use the Internet to take a closer look at the colleges you're interested in. You might be able to find out a lot of information before you consider going for a visit. You can look up nondiscrimination policies, peruse majors and course listings, find out about student groups (including whether there's one for GLBTQ people), and learn more about the areas where the colleges are located.

Check out a "best colleges" guide. One of the best-known is the *U.S. News and World Best Colleges* guide. *The Advocate College Guide for LGBT Students* is a queer-specific guide that offers a list of the 100 best schools in the country for queer students.

Perhaps the most up-to-date and easily accessible resource is the online Campus Climate Index (www.campusclimateindex .org). This site is operated by Campus Pride, a national non-profit group for student leaders and campus groups that works to create more GLBTQ-friendly environments at colleges and universities. The Campus Climate Index includes reviews and ratings of colleges, ranking how GLBTQ-friendly they are. It also includes information on size, degree offerings, tuition, and financial aid resources for GLBTQ students.

Investigate your colleges of choice. What if you have your heart set on a school that doesn't have high marks for being GLBTQ-friendly? Just because a school hasn't earned an official queer-friendly designation doesn't mean it isn't good for GLBTQ students. Here are some ways to find out if the schools you're interested in are queer-friendly.

- **Get a copy of the school's nondiscrimination policy.** All colleges should have one. Look in the student handbook or an admissions guidebook. It might even be posted at the website. If you see "sexual orientation" and (hopefully) "gender identity" as categories protected from discrimination, that's a good sign. If those words aren't there, you might not have any recourse if you become a victim of harassment or discrimination by the college or its students.

BEEN THERE

"I was out to my closest friends from home. As a college freshman, I was re-closeted. I didn't have anyone to talk to and just felt lost. I finally found the on-campus Alliance and have been active ever since. This year I am the copresident — I'm out to my whole campus now." —Cathy, 20

- **Investigate the campus climate.** Does the campus have a GLBTQ student group? Is it active? Some campuses even have queer resource or community centers.
- **Talk to students.** If a GLBTQ group or GSA is on campus, contact the organization to talk with one or more of the students. Most of these groups are happy to help.

GLBTQ Campus Directory (www.lgbtcampus.org/directory). To find a listing of schools with staff dedicated to GLBTQ resources, visit the website of the Consortium of Higher Education LGBT Resource Professionals.

- **Check out the curriculum.** If a school includes queer studies or similar curriculum, or even a few courses such as gender anthropology or gay and lesbian history, chances are it's a pretty friendly place (at least academically). Although entire queer studies programs or majors aren't commonplace yet, many schools have one or more classes on topics like queer theory or gender in society. Departments like English, political science, sociology, and theater also are frequently home to courses on queer topics. A lot of the class information should be available online. You can also call the school and ask to speak with someone in a particular department or in an academic administrator's office.

  It helps to remember that the college that's right for you includes many factors, not the least of which is academics. If a college doesn't have the courses you're interested in or the major you want, it's not going to be a great match for you even if it does appear to be queer-friendly or have an "official" queer-friendly designation.

Check out the surrounding area. When you leave for college, unless you're sticking close to home, you're also moving to another community. You'll want to do some investigating into that area to find out if it's GLBTQ-friendly. You don't have to go to school in a city to be in a queer-friendly area. Many schools in suburban and rural areas are friendly, too.

Visit the schools you're most interested in. If you can, visit the schools you're most interested in attending. You can learn a lot on a campus visit that guidebooks, college materials, and guidance counselors don't cover. This might be a good time to explore the GLBTQ resource or community center or meet people in the school's queer group. Even if you can't do that, simple things like eating in a dining hall, reading the flyers on campus bulletin boards, and looking through the campus newspaper (which may also be online) can tell you a lot about a school's culture and quality of life. Pay attention to how you feel being on campus. Do you feel comfortable, or are certain things making you nervous? This is all information you can use when it comes time to decide where you're going to college.

Fraternities and Sororities

Many GLBTQ people are members of a sorority or fraternity. In fact, Delta Lambda Phi is a fraternity that bills itself as being "for gay, bisexual, and progressive men." You can visit the website of this organization (www.dlp.org) for more information. Other Greek organizations bill themselves as queer-friendly, although some of this depends on the particular campus more than the parent organization. The Lambda 10 Project is a group for GLBTQ Greek organizations and addresses a variety of issues that can be part of being Greek and queer. Its website (www.lambda10.org) also features news and resources and hosts a bulletin board and chat room for GLBTQ Greeks. Information on how to help your campus organizations become more queer-friendly also is available. The point is, if you dream of being a sorority chick or a frat daddy, you don't have to give that up because you're queer.

BEEN THERE

"Some friends and I at the University of Virginia felt that, while there are a number of GLBTQ groups on campus, there weren't enough options for GLBTQ students in terms of fraternities and sororities. There are several national gay fraternities and a handful of lesbian sororities, but neither had any local chapters. So we decided to start our own fraternity — Sigma Omicron Rho (SOR). To the best of my knowledge, SOR is the only gender-neutral queer fraternal collegiate organization in the country.

"We seek to provide a semi-traditional Greek experience and the camaraderie that comes with it for queer, allied, and gender nonconforming students who otherwise would not feel comfortable pledging a fraternity or sorority. We never ask any of our members to identify in any way — we are totally inclusive regardless of whether you're GLBTQ or straight. It's amazing because we truly feel that all of our members value and care for one another on a personal level. I was literally moved to tears at an event last semester when I looked around and realized that the very existence of SOR had touched people's lives in a very real way." —Meredith, 21

Going with the Flow:
Some Thoughts on Getting Older

Leaving high school is a big transition for all teens. For GLBTQ teens, it can be the gateway to a whole new world. With increased independence, you'll most likely have greater access to other GLBTQ people, especially if you move to an urban area. You may discover a completely different social world, which can be exhilarating, frightening, and a big relief. You'll finally have more control over your environment than you did when you were in high school.

You might find that all of the experiences you had up through high school—even the really difficult ones—helped make you a pretty strong and amazing person.

All of this change and transition makes for an exciting time. It can be tempting to do everything you weren't able to do before, like spend most of your time socializing, dating, and going out. With the sudden increase in access to a whole new community, it can be easy to get carried away. The same instincts that helped you take care of yourself and keep it together until graduation are still valuable to you.

Trust yourself to make the decisions that are best for you. Even though the scenery and the people might have changed, your instincts haven't. So explore and discover new ideas and people, and most of all, enjoy yourself and your life. You deserve it.

BEEN THERE
"The best thing about being GLBTQ is that there is so much diversity in the community. There is so much more than being GLBTQ that makes us who we are, it's just one thing that brings us together. We know how not to be judgmental of others and we grow together. When one person in this community does something positive it affects everyone, and that is important. We always move one step forward, together." — Yvonne, 20

Glossary

A word about words. Some people are offended by the use of words like *queer, dyke,* and *fag* because they once had extremely negative connotations and were primarily used as insults. These words have been reclaimed or "taken back" by many in the GLBTQ community. Now, many GLBTQ people use words like queer, dyke, and fag as a means of asserting pride in who they are.

As you read this glossary, keep in mind that the language of the GLBTQ community is always changing. Words aren't always perfect, or even as exact as we would like them to be, but without them we wouldn't be able to talk about GLBTQ issues. And talking about queerness is one of the most important things we can do.

ally: Someone who supports GLBTQ people. Allies often help and provide visible and vocal support to stop bullying by reporting incidents. Group members in gay-straight alliances are allies.

anatomy: The physical characteristics of the body, often used in reference to a specific sex. An anatomical male has a penis and testicles. An anatomical female has a vagina, a vulva, ovaries, a clitoris, and breasts. People whose anatomy doesn't match their gender identity are called transgender.

androgyne, also gender bender and gender blender: People who are androgynous or who are gender bender/blenders merge what are stereotypically male and female characteristics in many different ways. Some are subtle and some can be considered shocking. Someone who is androgynous may not be obviously male or female at first glance (or even second or third glance). There are also people who blend genders, for example, "riot grrls" might shave their heads and wear combat boots, but also wear makeup and a skirt. Being androgynous or a gender bender is not necessarily a reflection of sexual orientation or gender identity.

asexual: A lack of sexual feelings toward men and women.

bisexual: A person who is emotionally, romantically, and sexually attracted to people of either sex.

biological sex: The sex someone is born as. Also referred to as *birth sex, anatomical sex,* and *physical sex.*

butch: A term used to describe both males and females who act and dress in stereotypically masculine ways.

closeted: A person who does not disclose his or her sexual orientation or gender identity. People may also be partially closeted—only coming out to a select few.

coming out: Disclosing one's sexual orientation or gender identity to others. Some people never come out, others come out to a few individuals, others are out to everyone, and for some, the coming out process takes place more slowly.

crossdresser: Crossdressers are people who dress in the clothing of the opposite sex. They may do this in private or in public. Crossdressers used to be called transvestites. They can be male or female and can be straight, gay, lesbian, or bisexual.

drag queens and drag kings: Drag queens (men who dress as women) and drag kings (women who dress as men) usually present larger than life representations of men and women. They exaggerate stereotypes of men and women, usually for entertainment. Dressing as a drag queen or king is not necessarily a reflection of sexual orientation or gender identity. Drag queens or kings can be GLBTQ or straight, they may be crossdressers, or they may just dress as the opposite sex when they are entertaining.

ex-gay movement: This movement attempts to convert people who are GLBTQ to being straight. Members encourage queer people to undergo conversion or reparative therapy. The ex-gay movement has been discredited by major medical organizations in the United States who have declared that being queer isn't a choice and cannot be changed.

femme: A term used to describe both males and females who act and dress in stereotypically feminine ways.

FTM, also F-T-M and F2M: Stands for female-to-male. Refers to transgender people who were born with female bodies but have a predominantly male gender identity. They may express this with their appearance (clothes, hair, etc.) or they may opt for a physical change that can involve hormones and/or surgery.

gay: This term is often used to describe both homosexual men and homosexual women, though it is more commonly used to refer to homosexual men. As it refers to men, gay describes men who are emotionally, romantically, and sexually attracted to other men. The word gay didn't come into wide use to describe homosexual people until the 1950s. Before that, it was used as a code word for same-sex sexuality.

gay-straight alliance (GSA): A student club for gay, lesbian, bisexual, transgender, and questioning students as well as their straight allies. GSAs can provide a social haven and support for queer students. They can also work for positive change on GLBTQ issues within a school or school system. GSAs are legally entitled to exist according to a federal court ruling.

gender: While this word may be used to describe anatomy, it's really about a person's identity as feminine or masculine rather than the physical characteristics that make someone female or male. Gender is made up of many things, including behaviors, cultural characteristics, and psychological traits that are associated with a specific sex.

gender dysphoria: A term for the pain, anxiety, and confusion that can result when there is a disparity between a person's gender identity and biological sex. Pressure to conform to accepted gender roles and expression, and a general lack of acceptance from society, also contribute to it.

gender expression: How you express your gender identity. It includes your clothes, hairstyle, body language (how you walk, your posture, your gestures, your mannerisms), and even speech patterns. In society, people often take their cues from someone's gender expression to decide that person's anatomical sex.

gender identity: Your internal sense of being male or female—it's whether you consider or feel yourself to be male or female. A person's gender identity doesn't necessarily reflect her or his biological sex. It's possible to have a gender identity that is male, female, or something else entirely.

gender identity disorder (GID): Mental health professionals often diagnose transgender people with GID. A diagnosis of GID lets transgender people get mental and physical treatment, which can be especially helpful for people trying to physically transition their gender. But a diagnosis of GID can also carry the stigma of mental illness.

genderqueer, also intergender and gender-variant: This term describes people whose gender identities exist outside of the traditional male and female binary. Those who identify as genderqueer may identify as male and female, neither, or just "other." These people also express gender in a variety of ways.

gender transitioning: Gender transitioning is a complex, multi-step process of starting to live in a way that accurately reflects a transgender person's true gender identity. Transitioning primarily involves social behaviors such as changing your name, dressing differently, altering other aspects of your appearance like hair or makeup, and changing your mannerisms, your voice, and how you move. Transitioning doesn't, by definition, include surgery or other physical changes, though it may depending on the person. A physical transition might include taking hormones or other substances under the supervision of a medical professional. For some, transitioning also involves surgery.

GLBTQ: An acronym that stands for gay, lesbian, bisexual, transgender, and questioning.

heterosexism: The idea that heterosexual people are the norm and that GLBTQ people are somehow abnormal; the assumption that people are heterosexual. Heterosexism contributes to homophobia.

heterosexual: People who are emotionally and physically attracted to people of the opposite sex.

homophobia: Homophobia is when someone feels a negative emotion like fear, anger, or suspicion toward someone for being GLBTQ. Homophobia can also take the form of ignorance about queer people. Homophobia can be very overt, like someone shouting "dyke!" or "fag!" in the hall, or it can be subtle, like a teammate quietly trying to avoid being near you in the locker room.

homosexual: People who are emotionally and physically attracted to people of the same sex.

intersex: People who are born with a mixture of both male and female genitals or with ambiguous genitalia. In many cases, the doctor or parents "choose" the child's anatomy and the child has a series of surgeries throughout infancy and childhood to definitively assign one anatomical sex. The surgery doesn't always result in a physical sex assignment that matches the person's internal gender. As a result, some intersex people grow up having gender identity issues that mirror those experienced by transgender people.

lesbian: A woman who is emotionally, romantically, and sexually attracted to other women.

MTF, also M-T-F and M2F: Stands for male-to-female. Refers to people who were born with male bodies but who have a predominantly female gender identity. They might express this with their appearance (clothes, hair, etc.) or they may opt for a physical change that can involve the use of hormones and possibly surgery.

omnisexual: See *pansexual.*

out: Living openly as a queer person. When GLBTQ people tell other people that they are queer, the process is called "coming out," as in "coming out of the closet." Being outed is when someone accidentally or purposefully reveals another person's sexual orientation or gender identity, often before that person is ready to do so.

pansexual, also omnisexual: Pansexual and omnisexual are terms used to identify sexual orientation. Those who identify in this way may be emotionally, romantically, and sexually attracted to people of either biological sex or gender expression.

passing: The ability to be accepted in society as someone of a different biological sex. Being able to pass is important for many transgender people, especially those who want to completely transition physically. They have to undergo a Real-Life Experience where they live as their correct gender identity for a period of time, usually one year, before the surgery is performed.

queer: Refers to people who are gay, lesbian, bisexual, transgender, or questioning. Sometimes used as a slur, the term has been reclaimed by many GLBTQ people who use it as an expression of pride. Some GLBTQ people prefer to identify as queer rather than gay, lesbian, bisexual, or transgender, because they feel it encompasses more of who they are or gives a greater sense of unity with the entire community.

questioning: Being uncertain of one's sexual orientation or gender identity.

sex reassignment surgery (SRS): In sex reassignment surgery, a surgeon modifies the primary sex characteristics (the genitals). Some transsexuals who need a complete physical transformation undergo SRS in conjunction with hormone therapy. It is sometimes accompanied by surgeries on secondary sex characteristics as well (breasts, Adam's apple) or cosmetic surgery.

sexual behavior: Sexual behavior only describes sexual activity, not sexual identity. For example, a man may identify as gay but still engage in sexual behavior with women. That's still considered heterosexual behavior. Or a woman may not identify as a lesbian but she may take part in sexual activity with a woman. That is homosexual behavior.

sexual identity: How a person views and identifies himself or herself in terms of his or her sexual orientation or behavior. Some people may identify as gay, lesbian, bisexual, or straight; other people may refuse to identify with a particular label. Some GLBTQ people choose to identify as queer for this reason. An individual's sexual identity is decided by that person, so a person who participates in straight sexual behavior may still identify as gay, lesbian, or bisexual and vice versa. A person's sexual identity can change over the course of his or her life.

sexual orientation: A term used to describe who someone is emotionally, romantically, and sexually attracted to. Gay, lesbian, bisexual, and straight all describe different forms of sexual orientation. Sexual orientation—and being queer—isn't just about who you have sex with. Because of that there have been suggestions for a more accurate phrase such as "emotional orientation" or "affectional orientation." But for now, sexual orientation is the common phrase.

straight: Synonymous with *heterosexual.*

transgender: When you're transgender, you have a gender identity or gender expression that is different from your biological sex or physical anatomy. Transgender is a broad term that covers many groups. It can include transsexuals (in all stages), drag kings and queens, crossdressers, people who are intersex, and others. People who are trans may identify themselves in a variety of ways. Being transgender isn't a reflection of sexual orientation. Transgender people are often straight, but they can also be gay, lesbian, or bisexual.

transitioning: See gender transitioning.

transphobia: Transphobia is when someone feels a negative emotion like fear, anger, or suspicion toward someone else for being transgender. Transphobia can also take the form of ignorance about transgender people.

transsexual: Often used interchangeably with *transgender,* though there has been some controversy over this. Generally it refers to people who don't identify with the sex they were born and who may change their bodies through hormones and possibly surgery to reconcile gender identity and physical sex. All transsexuals are transgender, but not all transgender people are transsexuals.

Two Spirit: Certain Native American cultures described transgender people as having "two spirits." Generally Two-Spirit people were born into one sex but took on the gender roles for both sexes (though this definition varies somewhat across cultures). Today, some transgender people identify as Two Spirit.

Resources

It's nearly impossible to create an exhaustive list of all of the great GLBTQ resources available, and the list continues to expand. This information is intended to give you an idea of what's available and to provide you with starting points to explore a variety of topics.

Additional resources, as well as more detailed explanations of many of the entries here, can be found throughout this book. The Selected Bibliography on pages 215–218 also includes materials that may be of interest.

Books, Films, Publications

Bornstein, Kate. *Gender Outlaw: On Men, Women, and the Rest of Us*. New York: Vintage Books, 1995. Check out Kate Bornstein's book for an entertaining and thought-provoking discussion of what gender is and what it means to be differently gendered.

Cobain, Bev. *When Nothing Matters Anymore: A Survival Guide for Depressed Teens*. Minneapolis: Free Spirit Publishing, 2007. *When Nothing Matters Anymore* provides information on recognizing depression, getting help, and staying well. Full of helpful information and resources, the book also features stories from teens.

Corinna, Heather. *S.E.X.: The All-You-Need-to-Know Progressive Sexuality Guide to Get You Through High School and College*. New York: Marlowe, 2007. This plain-spoken guide offers credible information on some topics you might be a little reluctant to speak about with parents or friends.

Duberman, Martin, Martha Vicinus, and George Chauncey Jr., eds. *Hidden from History: Reclaiming the Gay & Lesbian Past*. New York: Plume, 1990. This book is a collection of 30 essays exploring same-sex relationships in different cultures and eras. Essays cover women who passed as men in 19th-century America, lesbian sexuality in certain Native American cultures, and other topics.

Duberman, Martin. *Stonewall*. New York: Dutton, 1993. Duberman's book provides historical information on the people who were involved in the Stonewall uprising and the early years of the Gay Liberation Movement.

Gray, Mary. *Out in the Country: Youth, Media, and Queer Visibility in Rural America*. New York: New York University Press, 2009. In this book, author Mary Gray discusses the diverse lives and experiences of rural gay teens.

Heron, Ann. *Two Teenagers in Twenty: Writings by Gay and Lesbian Youth*. Boston: Alyson Publications, 1994. First-person accounts by gay and lesbian teens about discovering one's sexual orientation, coming out to family and friends, and challenges queer people can face.

Jennings, Kevin, with Pat Shapiro. *Always My Child: A Parent's Guide to Understanding Your Gay, Lesbian, Bisexual, Transgender or Questioning Son or Daughter*. New York: Simon & Schuster, 2003. Written by the executive director of GLSEN, this friendly, thorough, and practical guide helps parents or guardians trying to understand their queer or questioning child.

Porter, Darwin, and Danforth Prince. *Fifty Years of Queer Cinema: 500 of the Best GLBTQ Films Ever Made*. Staten Island, NY: Blood Moon Productions, 2010. An anthology of queer people in film, this resource includes discussion of how GLBTQ people influenced some of the most popular movies of all time.

Rupp, Leila J. *A Desired Past: A Short History of Same-Sex Love in America*. Chicago: University of Chicago Press, 1999. This book provides a broad introduction to same-sex love in the United States and covers 400 years of these relationships.

Russo, Vito. *The Celluloid Closet: Homosexuality in the Movies*. New York: Harper & Row, 1987. Revised edition. This is a groundbreaking look at how queer people have been depicted in movies throughout the history of film.

Stein, Mark, ed. *Encyclopedia of Lesbian, Gay, Bisexual and Transgender History in America*. New York: Charles Scribner's Sons/Thomson/Gale, 2004. This three-volume encyclopedia provides a detailed history of queer people in the United States.

Covering all aspects of cultural, political, and social life, the resource provides a comprehensive look at GLBTQ heritage.

Stryker, Susan. *Transgender History*. Berkeley, CA: Seal Press, 2008. This history provides a comprehensive look at transgender people living in the United States from the 20th century to today.

Teaching Tolerance. *Bullied: A Student, a School and a Case That Made History* documentary and viewer's guide. Montgomery, AL: Southern Poverty Law Center, 2010. This educational kit, available for free to every U.S. school, chronicles a student's ordeal with anti-gay bullying and offers an inspiring message of hope to those fighting harassment (www.tolerance.org/bullied).

Xavier, Jessica, Courtney Sharp, and Mary Boenke. *Our Trans Children*. Washington, DC: PFLAG Transgender Network, 1998. This is a helpful booklet full of detailed information for anyone who wants to know more about being transgender. Also available as a free download.

Organizations

Advocates for Youth
2000 M Street NW, Suite 750
Washington, DC 20036
(202) 419-3420
www.advocatesforyouth.org
Advocates for Youth is an organization that helps young people make informed and responsible decisions about their reproductive and sexual health. The group's website also includes information on sexuality, spirituality, relationship abuse, and queer harassment.

American Civil Liberties Union (ACLU)
125 Broad Street, 18th Floor
New York, NY 10004
(212) 549-2500
www.aclu.org
The ACLU works in the courts to defend civil liberties for all people. Check out the website for information on a wide range of GLBTQ issues, including safe school initiatives and same-sex relationship legislation.

Gay & Lesbian Alliance Against Defamation (GLAAD)
104 West 29th Street, 4th Floor
New York, NY 10001
(212) 629-3322
www.glaad.org
GLAAD works to promote fair, accurate, and inclusive representations of GLBTQ people and events in newspapers, magazines, movies, television shows, and other media. Visit the group online for news on its latest advocacy efforts.

Gay and Lesbian Medical Association (GLMA)
459 Fulton Street, Suite 107
San Francisco, CA 94102
(415) 255-4547
www.glma.org
GLMA is an association of gay and lesbian medical professionals who provide referrals to queer-friendly physicians and health agencies. The group can help connect you with local medical providers who are respectful and supportive of GLBTQ people.

Gay, Lesbian and Straight Education Network (GLSEN)
90 Broad Street, 2nd Floor
New York, NY 10004
(212) 727-0135
www.glsen.org
GLSEN works to create safe schools for GLBTQ students. The organization offers information about national efforts to create queer-friendly classrooms as well as resources you can use to take action and create a gay-straight alliance in your school.

Hetrick-Martin Institute
2 Astor Place
New York, NY 10003
(212) 674-2400
www.hmi.org
The Hetrick-Martin Institute has a wide variety of programs for GLBTQ people ages 12 to 21 in the New York City area. While programs are not nationwide, the institute's website is a good source of information for queer young people.

Human Rights Campaign (HRC)
1640 Rhode Island Avenue NW
Washington, DC 20036
1-800-777-4723
www.hrc.org
HRC works to protect the rights of GLBTQ people. The organization's website includes information on National Coming Out Day, safe schools, workplace equality, queer-related legislation, and many other issues.

Lambda Legal
120 Wall Street, Suite 1500
New York, NY 10005
(212) 809-8585
www.lambdalegal.org
Lambda Legal works to protect the civil rights of people who are GLBTQ. Visit the website to learn about its advocacy efforts, and use the interactive map to see how well your state protects the rights of queer people.

National Gay and Lesbian Task Force (NGLTF)
1325 Massachusetts Avenue NW, Suite 600
Washington, DC 20005
(202) 393-5177
www.ngltf.org
NGLTF has advocated for GLBTQ rights for more than three decades. It is a good resource if you experience harassment or discrimination for being queer. Among its many services are referrals to attorneys, physicians, counselors, and other professionals.

National Youth Advocacy Coalition (NYAC)
1638 R Street NW, Suite 300
Washington, DC 20009
1-800-541-6922
www.nyacyouth.org
NYAC is a social justice organization advocating for GLBTQ teens. Its mission is to end discrimination and improve the physical and emotional health of queer young people. Visit the website for information on a wide range of GLBTQ issues.

Parents, Families and Friends of Lesbians and Gays (PFLAG)
1828 L Street NW, Suite 660
Washington, DC 20036
(202) 467-8180
www.pflag.org
This national organization has more than 500 affiliates across the
United States. With a membership of more than 200,000, it is one
of the largest and most influential GLBTQ groups in the country.
PFLAG's website features information supporting queer people
and their families.

Sexual Minority Youth Assistance League (SMYAL)
410 7th Street SE
Washington, DC 20003
(202) 546-5940
www.smyal.org
For more than 25 years, this organization has been supporting
the health of young GLBTQ people. Offering outreach programs
in the Washington, D.C., metro area, SMYAL also provides
advocacy information at its website.

Hotlines

Boys Town National Hotline
1-800-448-3000
The Boys Town National Hotline is available 24-7 for both male
and female teens in need of help. Professional counselors staff
the hotline and can provide advice on any issue, including
depression, suicide, and identity struggles. More information is
available online (www.boystown.org).

GLBT National Hotline
1-888-THE-GLNH (1-888-843-4564)
This hotline is staffed by counselors Monday through Friday
from 4 p.m. to midnight and Saturday from noon to 5 p.m.
eastern standard time. Staff provides crisis counseling, referrals,
shelter listings, and other information. You can also visit the
GLBT National Help Center's website (www.glnh.org) for peer-
support chats.

National Hopeline Network
1-800-SUICIDE (1-800-784-2433)
The National Hopeline Network is for people who are depressed or suicidal, or who are concerned about someone who is. The hotline connects callers to local crisis centers where trained counselors offer help at any time of day or night. Learn more at the Hopeline website (www.hopeline.com).

National Runaway Switchboard Hotline
1-800-RUNAWAY (1-800-786-2929)
This hotline provides information for teens who have or are planning to run away from home. It also provides information and referrals for other crisis situations, including home violence, drug or alcohol abuse, and depression. The website (www.1800runaway.org) also has information available.

Rape, Abuse and Incest National Network (RAINN) National Sexual Assault Hotline
1-800-656-HOPE (1-800-656-4673)
This hotline offers crisis support and referrals for those who have been sexually assaulted. Victims of abuse can call whether an attack took place recently or a long time ago. Advice and resources are also available online (www.rainn.org).

The Trevor Lifeline
1-866-4-U-Trevor (1-866-488-7386)
This 24-7 hotline sponsored by the The Trevor Project is for GLBTQ teens who are depressed or just need someone to talk to. Trained counselors can offer advice on any issues you're facing and connect you with other resources. You can submit questions via email at the website (www.thetrevorproject.org).

Websites
Go Ask Alice!
www.goaskalice.com
While not specifically for GLBTQ teens, this website features reliable information about sexuality, relationships, and health issues. Experts provide advice in response to questions posted by site visitors. You can read old posts or ask a question of your own.

It Gets Better Project
www.itgetsbetter.org
It's an unfortunate reality that many people still are homophobic, but this website, featuring videos from queer teens and supporters, can help you remember that plenty of accepting, open-minded people also are out there.

Lesbian, Gay, Bisexual, and Transgender Health
www.cdc.gov/lgbthealth
Maintained by the Centers for Disease Control, this site features GLBTQ-specific advice on sexuality and health for people who are queer. Visit for accurate information and links to additional resources.

National Council on Alcoholism and Drug Dependence
www.ncadd.org
Unfortunately, GLBTQ teens are more likely to use drugs and alcohol than their straight peers. If you're using any of these dangerous (and illegal) substances, it's important to get help. This site provides treatment referrals and other useful information.

Oasis Magazine
www.oasisjournals.com
This online magazine is written by and for GLBTQ teens. Articles and advice columns at the site cover a wide range of important queer issues. It also has a forum where you can connect with other teens.

Scarleteen
www.scarleteen.com
Check out this website for nonjudgmental and accurate information about sex. Scarleteen features hundreds of articles as well as archived answers to visitors' questions. The site also features message boards and referral services.

YouthResource
www.amplifyyourvoice.org/youthresource
Check out this site by and for GLBTQ teens to get information on all kinds of issues, including queer advocacy, sexual health, relationships, and spirituality. It also features stories of other teens and links to other helpful resources.

Selected Bibliography

American Academy of Pediatrics. "Suicide and Suicide Attempts in Adolescents." Committee on Adolescence. *Pediatrics, 120, No. 3* (September 2007): 669–676.

"Answers to Your Questions for a Better Understanding of Sexual Orientation and Homosexuality." Washington, DC: American Psychological Association, 2008.

Austin, S. B., N. Ziyadeh, L. B. Fisher, J. A. Kahn, G. A. Colditz, and A. L. Frazier. "Sexual Orientation and Tobacco Use in a Cohort Study of U.S. Adolescent Girls and Boys." *Archives of Pediatric Adolescent Medicine, 158* (2004): 317–322.

Ayyar, Raj. "George Weinberg: Love Is Conspiratorial, Deviant & Magical." *GayToday.com.* November 1, 2002.

Benizet-Lewis, Benoit. "Coming Out in Middle School." *The New York Times Magazine.* September 23, 2009.

Bornstein, Kate. *Gender Outlaw: On Men, Women, and the Rest of Us.* New York: Vintage Books, 1995.

Centers for Disease Control. "Physical Dating Violence Among High School Students—United States, 2003." *Morbidity and Mortality Weekly Report, 55, No. 19* (2006): 532–535.

Centers for Disease Control. "Youth Risk Behavior Surveillance—United States, 2009." *Morbidity and Mortality Weekly Report, 59, No. SS-5* (2010).

Cianciotto, Jason, and S. Cahill. "Youth in the Crosshairs: The Third Wave of Ex-Gay Activism." New York: National Gay and Lesbian Task Force Policy Institute, 2006.

Clements-Nolle K., R. Marx, and M. Katz. "Attempted Suicide Among Transgender Persons: The Influence of Gender-Based Discrimination and Victimization." *Journal of Homosexuality, 51, No. 3* (2006): 53–69.

"Coming Out About Smoking: A Report from the National LGBTQ Young Adult Tobacco Project." National Youth Advocacy Coalition, 2010.

"Corporate Equality Index: A Report Card on Lesbian, Gay, Bisexual, and Transgender Equality in Corporate America." Washington, DC: Human Rights Campaign Foundation, 2010.

"The Cost of Harassment: A Fact Sheet for Lesbian, Gay, Bisexual, and Transgender High School Students." American Civil Liberties Union. February 9, 2007.

Duberman, Martin, Martha Vicinus, and George Chauncey Jr., eds. *Hidden from History: Reclaiming the Gay & Lesbian Past.* New York: Penguin Group, 1989.

Earls, Meg. "GLBTQ Youth." Washington, DC: Advocates for Youth, 2005.

"Facts for Features. Back to School: 2006–2007." Maryland: U.S. Census Bureau. www.census.gov/newsroom/releases/archives/facts_for_features_special_editions/cb06-ff11-2.html (accessed December 13, 2010).

Garafola, Nick. "Safe Zones for LGBTQ Teens." Sex, Etc. www.sexetc.org/story/lgbtq/5341. April 17, 2009 (accessed December 28, 2010).

"Global Facts and Figures." Geneva, Switzerland: Joint United Nations Programme on HIV/AIDS and World Health Organization, 2009.

Halpern, Carolyn, M. L. Young, M. W. Waller, et al. "Prevalence of Partner Violence in Same-Sex Romantic and Sexual Relationships in a National Sample of Adolescents." *Journal of Adolescent Health, 35* (2004): 124–131.

Halpern Carolyn, S. G. Oslak, M. L. Young, et al. "Partner Violence Among Adolescents in Opposite-Sex Romantic Relationships: Findings from the National Longitudinal Study of Adolescent Health." *American Journal of Public Health, 91, No. 10* (2001): 1679–1685.

"Hate Crimes Statistics, 2007." Washington, DC: Federal Bureau of Investigation, 2008.

"Health and Risk Behaviors of Massachusetts Youth, 2007: The Report." Massachusetts Department of Elementary and Secondary Education and Massachusetts Department of Public Health, May 2008.

Jackson, Tom. "NYCLU Sues Herkimer Co. School District for Failing to Protect Gay Youth from Harassment." *LGBT News.* August 19, 2009.

"Jump-Start Guide to Building and Activating Your GSA." Washington, DC: GLSEN, 2000.

Kosciw, Joseph, E. Diaz, and E. Greytak. "2007 National School Climate Survey: The Experiences of Lesbian, Gay, Bisexual and Transgender Youth in Our Nation's Schools." New York: GLSEN, 2008.

Lake, Celinda, and E. LeCouteur. "Talking About Respect: A+ Messages for Those Working to Create Safe Schools for Lesbian, Gay, Bisexual and Transgender Youth." New York: GLSEN, 2003.

"Lesbian, Gay, Bisexual and Transgender Domestic Violence in the United States in 2007: A Report of the National Coalition of Anti-Violence Programs." New York: National Coalition of Anti-Violence Programs, 2008.

Marshal, M. P., M. S. Friedman, R. Stall, K. M. King, J. Miles, M. A. Gold, O. G. Bukstein, and J. Q. Morse. "Sexual Orientation and Adolescent Substance Use: A Meta-Analysis and Methodological Review." *Addiction, 103* (2008): 546–556.

Newport, Frank. "This Easter, Smaller Percentage of Americans Are Christian: Americans More Likely Now Than in Previous Decades to Say They Have No Religious Identity." Gallup. April 10, 2009.

Pew Research Center for the People & the Press. "National Survey." Washington, DC, 2006.

"Questions and Answers: LGBTQ Youth Issues." New York: Sexuality Information and Education Council of the United States (SEICUS). www.siecus.org/index.cfm?fuseaction=page.vie wpage&pageid=605&grandparentID=477&parentID=591 (accessed December 13, 2010).

Pope H. G., A. J. Gruber, J. I. Hudson, M. A. Huestis, and D. Yurgelun-Todd. "Neuropsychological Performance in Long-Term Cannabis Users." *Archives of General Psychiatry, 58, No. 10* (2001): 909–915.

"Report of the Comprehensive Review of the Issues Associated with a Repeal of 'Don't Ask, Don't Tell.'" Washington, DC: Department of Defense. November 30, 2010.

Roberts, T. A., and J. Klein. "Intimate Partner Abuse and High-Risk Behavior in Adolescents." *Archives of Pediatrics & Adolescent Medicine, 157* (2003): 375–380.

Ryan, Caitlin, and Donna Futterman. *Lesbian and Gay Youth: Care & Counseling.* New York: Columbia University Press, 1998.

Saad, Lydia. "Americans Evenly Divided on Morality of Homosexuality." Gallup. June 18, 2008.

Savin-Williams, Ritch C. *The New Gay Teenager.* Cambridge: Harvard University Press, 2006.

"State of the Nation 2005: Challenges Facing STD Prevention Among Youth—Research, Review, and Recommendations." Research Triangle Park, NC: American Social Health Association, 2005.

"Transgender Americans: A Handbook for Understanding." Washington, DC: Human Rights Campaign Foundation, 2008.

"Transgender/SOFFA: Domestic Violence/Sexual Assault Resource Sheet." Milwaukee, WI: FORGE: For Ourselves: Reworking Gender Expression, undated.

Troiden, Richard. "The Formulation of Homosexual Identities." *Journal of Homosexuality,* 17 (1989): 43–73.

Varia, Smith, "Dating Violence Among Adolescents." Washington, DC: Advocates for Youth, 2006.

"Youth Knowledge and Attitudes on Sexual Health: A National Survey of Adolescents and Young Adults. Special analysis prepared for Dangerous Liaisons: Substance Abuse and Sexual Behavior, a one-day conference sponsored by the National Center on Addiction and Substance Abuse (CASA) at Columbia University." The Henry J. Kaiser Family Foundation and the National Institute on Drug Abuse, 2002.

Index

H

Happiness, 19

Harassment/bullying
cyberbullying, 45, 68
difference between, 34
feelings evoked by, 32, 35–36
homophobia and, 28
responding to
assessing situation, 36–37
cyberbullying, 45
documenting incidents, 43
with education, 41
examples of, 38, 39, 40–41
hotlines for, 47
with humor, 37
organizations to contact, 47
speaking up, 38–41
turning other cheek, 37
statistics, 68
suicide and, 28, 33

Harassment/bullying in schools
changing schools because of, 82–84
death threats, 69
examples of, 32, 33, 35–36
extent of, 33
lawsuits against, 32, 73
proposed legislation about, 81
responding to
contacting national organizations, 44–45
education promoting tolerance, 24, 34, 35, 73
GBLTQ Online High School, 35
GSAs, 68, 69, 73
hotlines for, 47
National Day of Silence, 74, 75
reporting to school administration, 43–44
safe schools movements, 34

Hate crimes
law against, 29
percent based on sexual orientation, 29

"Health and Risk Behaviors of Massachusetts Youth," 134

Helminiak, Daniel, 159

Helplines. See hotlines

Heron, Ann, 208

Heterosexism
described, 203
as norm, 30–31

Heterosexual, described, 203

Hetrick-Martin Institute, described and contact information, 210

Hidden from History (Duberman, Vicinus, and Chauncey Jr.), 10, 29, 207

HIV/AIDS
lack of cure, 122
myths about, 40, 120
transmission of, 126

Homophobia
degrees of, 28
described, 27, 28, 204
examples of, 32, 33, 35–36, 40–41
feelings evoked by, 32, 35–36
heterosexism and, 203
internalized by GLBTQ people, 30
internalizing, 28
invisibility and, 30mob mentality and, 31
organizations fighting, 31
responding to
assessing situation, 36–37
with education, 41
examples of, 38, 39, 40–41
GSAs in schools, 68, 69, 73
with humor, 37
reporting to school administration, 43–44
speaking up, 38–41
turning other cheek, 37
roots of, 29

Homosexuality
attitudes of Americans toward, 46, 137
as mental disorder, 170
as normal, 13

Homosexuals
defined, 204
myth of bisexuals as, 22

Hormones, 171–172, 186–187

Hotlines
abusive relationships, 105
for addiction, 143
for depression, 138
for harassment/bullying, 47
for runaways, 138, 213
suicide, 63, 138
for trans people, 188

HRC (Human Rights Campaign). See Human Rights Campaign (HRC)

Human Rights Campaign (HRC)
Coming Out Project, 54
described and contact information, 15, 47, 180, 211
employment rights information, 190, 194
legislation and, 31, 33, 193
understanding transgender issues, 167–168

Humor, responding to homophobia with, 37

I

Identity confusion, 17

IFGE (International Foundation for Gender Education), described and contact information, 180

Immorality and GLBTQ people, 24

Integrity, described and contact information, 157

Interfaith Alliance, described and contact information, 157

Intergender, described, 203

International Foundation for Gender Education (IFGE), described and contact information, 180

About the Author

Kelly Huegel is the director of public-private partnerships for a military medical foundation. Previously, she worked for the Metropolitan Washington, D.C., chapter of PFLAG, where she provided support and educational services for GLBTQ people and their families. Kelly has a special passion for working with teens and holds a degree in secondary education.

The author of two books and more than 50 published articles, Kelly received critical acclaim for her first book, *Young People and Chronic Illness,* as well as for the first edition of *GLBTQ* (both published by Free Spirit Publishing).

Kelly is also a licensed massage therapist and certified personal trainer. A dedicated athlete and martial artist, she holds a black belt in Tae Kwon Do and also trains in Jun Fan Jeet Kune Do, Kali, and other weapons techniques. She and her girlfriend live in suburban Washington, D.C., and travel as often as possible to their adopted home of Miami.

Do you have lots of ideas and opinions? Have you ever seen a book or website and thought, "I'd do that differently"?

Then we want to hear from you! We're looking for teens to be part of the **Free Spirit Teen Advisory Council.** You'll help us keep our books and other products current and relevant by letting us know what you think about things like design, art, and content.

Go to www.freespirit.com/teens to learn more and get an application.

Other Great Books from Free Spirit

Fighting Invisible Tigers
Stress Management for Teens
(Revised & Updated Third Edition)
by Earl Hipp

Research suggests that adolescents are affected by stress in unique ways that can increase impulsivity and risky behaviors. This book offers proven techniques that teens can use to deal with stressful situations in school, at home, and among friends. They'll find current information on how stress affects health and decision making and learn stress-management skills to handle stress in positive ways. Filled with interesting facts, student quotes, and fun activities, this book is a great resource for any teen who's said, "I'm stressed out!" For ages 11 & up.

144 pp.; softcover; 2-color illust.; 6" x 9"

Teen Cyberbullying Investigated
When Do Your Rights End and Consequences Begin?
by Thomas A. Jacobs, J.D.

Teen Cyberbullying Investigated presents a powerful collection of landmark court cases involving teens and charges of cyberbullying, which includes: sending insulting or threatening emails, text, or instant messages directly to someone; spreading hateful comments about someone through emails, blogs, or chat rooms; stealing passwords and sending out threatening messages using a false identity; and building a website to target specific people. Each chapter features the seminal case and resulting decision, asks readers whether they agree with the decision, and urges them to think about how the decision affects their lives. For ages 12 & up.

208 pp.; softcover; 6" x 9"

Interested in purchasing multiple quantities? Contact edsales@freespirit.com or call 1.800.735.7323 and ask for Education Sales.

Many Free Spirit authors are available for speaking engagements, workshops, and keynotes. Contact speakers@freespirit.com or call 1.800.735.7323.

For pricing information, to place an order, or to request a free catalog, contact:

Free Spirit Publishing Inc.
217 Fifth Avenue North • Suite 200 • Minneapolis, MN 55401-1299
toll-free 800.735.7323 • local 612.338.2068
fax 612.337.5050 • help4kids@freespirit.com• www.freespirit.com